Twitch Secrets: The Experts Guide To E

"A simple step-by-step process that ANY streamer can use to improve their viewers, followers & subscribers."

TWITCH
SECRETS

THE EXPERT'S GUIDE TO BECOME TWITCH PARTNER

TREVOR MCCOLLUM

Twitch Secrets: The Experts Guide To Become Twitch Partner

LEGAL NOTICE

The Publisher has strived to be as accurate and complete as possible in the creation of this report, notwithstanding the fact that he does not warrant or represent at any time that the contents within are accurate due to the rapidly changing nature of the Internet.

While all attempts have been made to verify information provided in this publication, the Publisher assumes no responsibility for errors, omissions, or contrary interpretation of the subject matter herein. Any perceived slights of specific persons, peoples, or organizations are unintentional.

In practical advice books, like anything else in life, there are no guarantees of income made. Readers are cautioned to reply on their own judgment about their individual circumstances to act accordingly.

This book is not intended for use as a source of legal, business, accounting or financial advice. All readers are advised to seek services of competent professionals in legal, business, accounting, and finance field.

You are encouraged to print this book for easy reading.

Affiliate & Earnings Disclaimer:

Per the FTC's recent policy update that requests we be transparent about any and all affiliate relations we may have in this book, you
should assume that any and all links in this book are affiliate links and if you go through them to make a purchase I will earn a commission. Keep in mind that I link these companies and their products because of their quality and not because of the commission I receive from your purchases. The decision is yours, and whether or not you decide to buy something is completely up to you

Twitch Secrets: The Experts Guide To Become Twitch Partner

Twitch secrets: The Experts Guide to become Twitch Partner
Published by Trevor McCollum

Copyright ©2021 TREVOR MCCOLLUM. All rights reserved.

No part of this book may be reproduced in any form or by any mechanical means, including information storage and retrieval systems without permission in writing from the publisher slash author , except by a reviewer who may quote passages in a review .

All images, logos, quotes, and trademarks including in this book are subject to use according to trademark and copyright laws of the United States of America.

MCCOLLUM, TREVOR, Author

TWITCH SECRETS: The experts guide to become twitch partner.

TREVOR MCCOLLUM

ISBN: **9798707229756**

All Rights reserved by TREVOR MCCOLLUM.

This book is printed in the United States of America.

Twitch Secrets: The Experts Guide To Become Twitch Partner

Table of Contents

Easy Steps on How to Start Streaming on Twitch, PS5, and Xbox Series X................1
How to stream on Twitch PS5..4
How to stream on Twitch Xbox Series X..5
How much money does twitch streamers make per sub?..6
How To Create An Attractive Character For Your Brand..8
How To Get Twitch Followers...14
Where to promote twitch stream, Marketing Your Brand...18
How To Make A Twitch Overlay...23
How To Livestream To Twitch On A PC...26
Streaming PC Specs...31
The Difference Between Twitch Streaming Vs. YouTube Streaming.......................41
What Type Of Content Creator Do You Want To Be?...44
Best Free Twitch Overlay To Use For Your Streams...47
Best Green Screens for Streamers..55
Best Lighting for Streaming...60
Best Twitch Panels to Use For Your Streams and Where to Get Them....................68
Dual PC Streaming Setup - Is It Worth It?..72
How do I IRL Twitch Stream?...77
How to Simultaneously Stream on Twitch and YouTube..83
How to Stream on Facebook Gaming..87
How to Subscribe on Twitch?..92
    Royalty-Free Music for Twitch...97

Twitch Secrets: The Experts Guide To Become Twitch Partner

Easy Steps on How to Start Streaming on Twitch, PS5, and Xbox Series X

Twitch is an online platform that allows gamers to build communities that share interests that are similar to theirs. Through Twitch, people who are streaming or gaming can broadcast their activities or gameplay to an audience made of fans and other subscribers. Through this sharing, the audience gets to watch and listen to the gamers as they play.

There are two versions of Twitch, the free version, and the paid version. Subscribers using the paid version enjoy smooth streaming without interruption from ad pop-ups. They also enjoy expansive streaming and features of storage.

For you to have the ability to start streaming on Twitch or to create your content for others to view, you have to follow the following steps.

Twitch Secrets: The Experts Guide To Become Twitch Partner

Create a Twitch account

The first step before you can start streaming on Twitch is to create an account. Study the community guidelines on the Twitch website and be conversant with them.

If you are using a computer to create your account, click on the section that's written: "sign up". You'll be required to fill out your details on the spaces left on the form that appears on your screen.

To create an account via mobile phones or other devices, you first have to download the app and install it on your gadgets and fill out the form.

Enable an authentication that's two-factor based

You have to set a two-factor authentication from your desktop secure settings in your Twitch account to broadcast. The authentication cannot be carried out through the phone, so you strictly must use a computer desktop or laptop.

Once you are logged in to your Twitch account, click on the security settings, then click on the section that allows you to enable 2FA. You can go on and use your mobile devices after that.

Put together, connect and set your gear up for action.

The most sensible thing to do in this case is to use as limited gear as possible while streaming. For example, you can opt to cast instead of using a webcam. Additionally, communicate to your audience by texting them instead of speaking through the microphone.

In other situations, you might be required to use the webcam and the microphone; hence you shouldn't entirely do away with the options.

Twitch Secrets: The Experts Guide To Become Twitch Partner

Software installation and connection to Twitch

For this step, if you are using a desktop to stream on Twitch, you should consider installing software decoders. OBS Studio, Streamable OBS, Vmix, and Xsplit are available software to choose from.

After installing software such as OBS Studio, choose the option to stream through it. This is done by choosing "Twitch" as the service option.

Add the visuals and the video or audio you intend to use

Add everything you intend to broadcast in OBS Studio as a "source." Examples of "sources" are the microphone, webcam, and the game you plan to play.

Choose the suitable streaming settings for your device.

Factors to consider when choosing your streaming settings are the power of your processor, the upload bandwidth, and the content type you wish to broadcast. High-quality broadcast requires high-quality settings.

After this step, choose the go-live option and start streaming on Twitch.

Twitch Secrets: The Experts Guide To Become Twitch Partner

How to stream on Twitch PS5

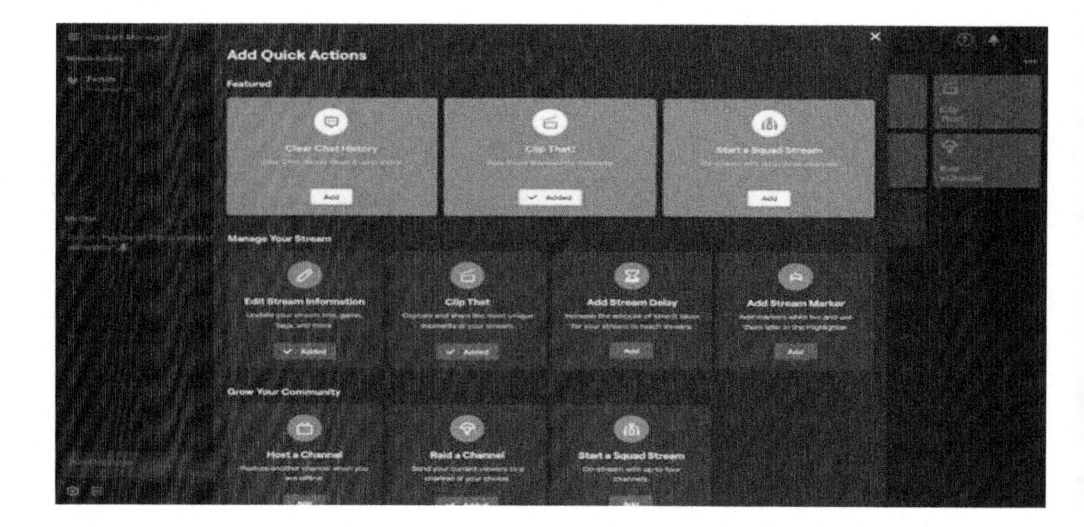

1. Create an account on Twitch using your computer or mobile devices

2. Write a bio and/or upload your photo on your account's wall so that other users and your audience can know who you are.

3. Sync your PlayStation Network to your account on Twitch by following the steps displayed on your screen, then input or scan the QR code as displayed.

4. Using your controller, press the option displayed as "create" while proceeding to play the game.

5. In the next step, select "Broadcast" from the options displayed, then select "Twitch."

6. The Broadcast option can also be selected from the control center you have customized in advance.

7. Write a title for your broadcast and finally click on the "Go Live" option to start streaming with your PS5.

Twitch Secrets: The Experts Guide To Become Twitch Partner

How to stream on Twitch Xbox Series X

1. Download the Twitch app and set up your account, uploading a photo and filling out your bio information for easier connection with your users.

2. Link your Xbox Series X account to your Twitch account by keying in the 6-digit code provided by the app.

3. Click on the "Broadcast" option and customize the settings for your broadcast. Choose options such as language, camera settings, your broadcast name, and the streaming resolution of your choice.

4. Select the "start streaming" option to begin streaming Twitch on Xbox Series X.

5. To choose the game, you wish to play, key in the "Xbox button" and wait for the guide to open. Go to " My games and apps," then to "see all."

6. Select your game of choice and start a live stream.

How much money does twitch streamers make per sub?

Twitch Secrets: The Experts Guide To Become Twitch Partner

The subscription levels differ, but all are done monthly. Twitch takes half of the subscription fee, implying that the broadcaster earns $2.50 or 12.50 per sub, depending on the subscription level.

Virtual cheers

These virtual cheers are called bits. Viewers purchase the bits that come in various sizes and colors for the chat window. Through this purchase, the streamer can earn some money. The viewers dole the subscriptions to their favorite streamers. The streamers receive a cut, which appearances a bit used in their chat.

As a twitch partner

This is the top tier for twitch users who want to become earners. Unlike the referral program, you must apply to qualify as a twitch partner. Partners earn more similarly to how affiliates do, but in addition to that, they get a share of ad revenue generated from their channel.

Twitch partner requirements:

- Broadcast for at least twenty-five hours in the st thirty days
- Stream for twelve unique days within the past thirty days
- Attain an average of seventy-five viewers in the past thirty days

Twitch Secrets: The Experts Guide To Become Twitch Partner

How To Create An Attractive Character For Your Brand

Now you've learned the streaming basics, and you have to learn how to establish your brand to keep your name growing. This process can be tricky, but it is worth it. You can't just depend on your streams to give you followers without branding and promoting your name to the win followers. People are not much different; everyone needs to create a magnetic and appealing brand to pull viewers and prosper.

However, most streamers don't know that they need to consider a few critical issues rather than merely creating an attractive character for a successful establishment of a personal brand. You might be thinking about better looks, no you're mistaken. Engaging personality here means the ability to compel more people to you, not necessarily by your physical appearances.

Twitch Secrets: The Experts Guide To Become Twitch Partner

Creating an attractive character can be tricky but exciting at the same time. Take your time and meditate on what makes you, your stream, or content unique and outstanding from the rest. After figuring out the uniqueness, then build on it.

Ensure your brand relates to your content

This means you should create a brand that relates to what you stream. If your channel is about fits and sorts, create brands revolving around the content. Moreover, build on what you love doing or are passionate about. If you can't determine if you have a persona or character necessary for building a channel, your viewers will help propel you in the right direction.

Begin small and work on expanding it

Building a brand is not an overnight thing; you have to take time and exercise patience. Humble beginnings will help to grow slowly but steadily and modify your brand. If the process is not done well, situations might need you to come back and redo. Moving steadily will save not only time but also money. Employ both strategic thinking and not rushing to avoid drawbacks in the future.

Utilize the branding categories

There are several ways you can use to express your channel brand on twitch. Ensure you mold your brand using the approaches; a strong brand should have several places that people can use to recognize and remember you. Make much of your webpage fit the story, beginning from channel names. Remember to blend this visual asset to match your channel brand when incorporating visual graphics such as custom emotes and on-screen alerts.

Elements of creating an attractive character

Building an attractive character has no links with personal looks or feelings but rather the ability to compel a crowd to your channel. The critical element to creating an engaging personality, according to Rusell Brunson, is because their audiences will

Twitch Secrets: The Experts Guide To Become Twitch Partner

follow you because they are through with the journey they are currently on and desire the result that you have achieved. The other way you can develop an attractive character is to become compelling when you attempt to do something yourself.

Backstory

When creating an attractive character, only share critical elements of your past story and have legitimate reasons for sharing it. Think of what you will achieve by sharing the story; maybe you share your success to motivate your audience, possibly revealing part of your life contributing to how you are today. Think of a challenge you overcame, and talk about it. The primary role of a back story is to humanize you; it gives your viewers a reason to follow you. It motivates and inspires them, which consoles them that they can start small and go big. The story gives them hope that nothing is impossible if they were as they are and have achieved much. They can attain their life goals.

Parables

Here it would help if you took your real-life story and relate it to your channel or business. Consider the actionable lessons you learned from your journey. Frame the experience into parables and share it with your audience. These experiences will offer the audience actual value. Take what you learned to make your audience's journey easier and help them achieve their goals.

Character flaws

No human is 100% perfect, so you should not portray yourself as excellent. Share your downfalls, mistakes, and flaws, and explain how you learned from them to be the strong person you are. Nobody is perfect, and all humans are prone to making mistakes, especially when trying new ideas. Use those imperfections or errors for your benefit. Sharing your mistakes will allow your viewers to get inside the real you.

They will believe in what you say rather than only show them your right side. In return, the audience will resonate more with you. Try as much as possible to avoid painting yourself as a perfect person who does mess. Prove to your viewers that you are human and you can mess. This will give them hope that they can as well achieve their goals.

Twitch Secrets: The Experts Guide To Become Twitch Partner

Polarity

Polarity is an influential factor in character branding. Don't be out to please anybody, because after all, not everyone will love you. Some will hate you, while others will like you no matter how pleasing you try to be. For a good connection with your audience, show them that you are not for everyone. Some people might not like nor follow you, and that is okay; that is life. Your followers will remain loyal and will purchase your products.

Identity

After tying the above four elements, then form your identity. Identity can be broken down into four components, from which you need to pick the one that fits you.

- The leader
- The crusader or the adventurer
- The reporter or the evangelist
- The reluctant hero

Storylines

Finally, develop storylines that can attract an audience and teach them how to attain their goals—stories from the best learning medium than any other type of information. The storyline is what links the four critical elements with identity.

Storyline options

- Redemption and loss
- Us vs. them
- Before and after

Twitch Secrets: The Experts Guide To Become Twitch Partner

- Amazing discovery
1. Secret telling
2. Third-person testimonial

The tagline or your handle

The tagline is an essential element in building an attractive character for your brand. Your handle is your tagline and is fairly crucial in brand marketing. Whatever selection on your handle is your choice, but it will most of the time depend on the services and goods you are trying to advertise. You can put several handles into use, for example, "the overnight success creator." Sign off your emails and sales in that manner. If you stream videos, remember to use a similar handle. The purpose of the handle is to make it easy for your audience to link you with what you stream. When your viewers think of you, they will associate your name with the handle.

Your personality

Here you don't have to be great; be entertaining. Include your details in your channel streaming; you can incorporate them in the chats with your viewers or any discussion with an audience. It is essential to weave your personal story into your branding, not looking at their form. The more appealing characters you can incorporate into your brand, the more the type of audience you can attract.

Use strong opinions

Apart from showing your flaws and mistakes, it is crucial to turn the coin and show your audience your strong side. Do not just give them your weaknesses. In other words, this means you should provide all-around information about yourself without majoring on one side. Weigh both sides, the strengths, and weaknesses, so that your audience can appeal to your story. It is alright to give your pet peeves, your quarks, and strong opinions. Understand that you can be boring if you stray neutral.

Twitch Secrets: The Experts Guide To Become Twitch Partner

Neutrality can lead to boredom for your audience, and you would have failed as a streamer out to the most out of your streaming. When you decide to be neutral, then be assured that nobody will listen to your streams. Try to share some aggressive or controversial opinions, share your views on the topic you know most people. Give contrary opinions on the subject; by doing so, you might not have many people agreeing or supporting them, but you will have many followers.

You have the idea and need to create an appealing character for your brand, but how do you share these elements as part of the attractive name? Utilize your emails, text messages, and any other marketing communication within your reach. Nowadays, several people share their personal information about their kids, pets, and private life to attract an audience to their channels. Remember, attention is money, so that they will generate money for you is when they pay attention to your content.

What you need to do now is to take your time, sit down and figure out what attractive character is in you and your streams. After doing so:

1. Decide on the backstory, parables, strong opinions, and character flaws you intend to share.
2. Most importantly, keep in mind the essence of polarity and the effects of neutrality.
3. Begin developing your appealing personality with an interesting backstory and weave it into all the marketing you do.

Twitch Secrets: The Experts Guide To Become Twitch Partner

How To Get Twitch Followers

Twitch is increasingly becoming a popular online place for content streaming. The platform has become one of the largest online video streaming platforms despite its newness. With a single month of launching, it has received more than eight million unique visitors. The numbers don't lie; this means that Twitch has an enormous and profitable audience awaiting you. Your only hassle to gout and get their attention. Suppose you wish to grow your twitch presence and reap the profits of being the most successful streamer, rock in here. Here are extensively researched and cherry-picked tips to help you win many followers' attention on your twitch account.

For any internet marketer who wants to make a name for themselves, one must know how to get twitch followers. It is an absolute must to know whether you have followers or not. If you don't have followers, you are not part of the internet marketing industry. On the other hand, if you have followers, you must know how to make them stick around.

Set SMART goals

If you want to benefit from Twitch's fantastic opportunities fully, it is imperative to treat your streaming like a business that needs goals, time, and dedication. Setting SMART goals and coming up with realistic strategies is an incredible way to go. You can use goal and gratitude planners to help you to organize your thoughts. Because your dream is to have several followers, your goals should focus on more viewers and subscribers.

Twitch Secrets: The Experts Guide To Become Twitch Partner

The more thought your plans will be, the more you will be assured that you will stick by them. Use the SMART framework to create meaningful goals to yield practical results. After setting your goals, then exercise patiently; you can't just expect overnight results. You have to be patient enough.

Be consistent with your streaming.

If you want a loyal follower from your audience, you should be consistent and frequent in streaming. It is easy, simple, and ideal to let your audience know when they can watch you. Coming up with a schedule and sharing it with your audience is an excellent way to build trust from your viewers, thus encouraging regular viewing. If you don't have a working schedule, it might be hard for your audience to know when to find you and follow consistent someone else.

Like the millions of people awaiting you, so is the competition; other streamers are competing for the followers, so setting up a schedule and adhering to it will put you on top of other competitors. Moreover, it is essential to include what you ought to present on the program to help your audience find an easy time finding the content they are looking for. As soon as you begin becoming consistent, your viewers will be expecting consistency, which will keep them loyal to viewing.

Value your audience

To attract the right kind of followers, you need to give value to your audience. This means that to attract your audience to visit your twitch page and view your streaming videos, you need to provide them with high-quality content that is of good value. You can do this by giving them updates on what is happening in your world and what new products you have created. This way, you not only entertain your audience, but you also promote your products. Hence, acquire the highest quality followers to get the best possible stream views on your streaming videos.

Be unique

With the numerous streamers online, only uniqueness can keep the ball rolling. Make your content unique from everybody else. The number of twitch followers you have will

Twitch Secrets: The Experts Guide To Become Twitch Partner

directly reflect the kind of online marketing strategies you have employed for your streams. This is because your business identity must be established within the social media realm. The internet is no place for passive online marketers. They must be proactive and put themselves into the social media scene to attract their audiences.

Make your stream channel visually appealing.

Besides an aesthetically appealing channel page, incorporate a neat and organized layout to help the audience find what they want. This will help in getting and retaining viewers, using graphically edited images that are visually attractive. The graphics will help make your channel look inviting and professional. Revamping your channel art, using images instead of text headlines, adding color, and expanding the description is a great way to optimize your chance to catch more viewers' attention visually.

To edit your channel's layout, log in to your account, go to the track, click on edit panels, and begin adding panels.

Use quality streaming equipment.

High-quality streaming equipment will ensure better interaction with your audience. Use equipment to ensure that your audience can see and hear you correctly. Invest in a good microphone and camera. A good camera will make your face and expressions clear to your audience. On the other hand, a good microphone will ensure that your audience will hear you, promoting a meaningful interaction.

Make fair use of social media.

It would be best to keep yourself at the forefront of your audience's mind by being a member of various social media networks such as Twitter, MySpace, Facebook, and others. These social media sites allow you to interact with your audience and provide them with updated information regarding the products you have created. This helps you build strong relations with your twitch followers and make them feel like you are one of their own.

Twitch Secrets: The Experts Guide To Become Twitch Partner

If you have an existing SMM account, it is best to link your Twitter account to your SMM. Linking these two accounts allows you to maximize the amount of audience that you can attract. If you already have an existing SMM account, it is best to create a button that allows your subscribers to join your Twitter account. Creating this button is very easy and is the first tip on how to get twitch followers.

Take Note!

One of the reasons many streamers have no followers is that they do not place the appropriate effort into promoting their channel. If you do not want to be left out of this growing community, you should dedicate time to promoting your channel. The more you promote your stream, the more viewers you will have. The last thing you want to do is continue to lose subscribers because you did not take the time to promote your channel.

The most important thing is to promote your product. When you create a channel on twitch, inform your viewers of the new channel you are creating. Please do not leave them hoping that something good will happen to your stream. Always give them fresh content that they can interact with. A good streamer always focuses on expanding their audience rather than their subscriber base.

Twitch Secrets: The Experts Guide To Become Twitch Partner

Where to promote twitch stream, Marketing Your Brand.

Social Media

As a streamer, you don't need to merely depend on what you broadcast on Twitch to give you success. You have to find other ways to gain the largest number of viewers and followers to benefit from your career because this is more of a business that needs dedication. The activities you undertake on other media sites play a crucial role in your channel's growth. Social media platforms are the best places ever you can advertise your streaming.

When you are new in the Twitch broadcasting stream, you might not have so many viewers; this calls for your efforts to sell your reputation out there and divert your audience's attention to your channel. The best approach to use is cross-promoting your site on relevant panels and social media. When you create more engagement, you will get more viewers, thus growing your audience. Therefore, remaining active on all platforms ensures more audience and more yield. Some of the media platforms you can use are:

Twitch Secrets: The Experts Guide To Become Twitch Partner

Twitter

Recently, Twitter is increasingly becoming a worldwide platform where people meet online. So, as a streamer, you can utilize this site by sharing some of your streams there. This will keep you in touch with your target audience; if you post some good and creative content, you will catch the attention of millions of Twitter users, hence diverting them all to your channel. Twitter's generation demographics skew to the current generation, and these young people have a keen enthusiasm for gaming; therefore, they are liable to be drawn to your game broadcast.

Additionally, Twitter has user-friendly options that allow users to design and post easily shared content. If one user sees the content, they can share it with other Twitter users efficiently. The sharing can promote traffic to the channel, increasing your viewers and audience. If you want to benefit more from this platform, include some pivotal elements to convert most Twitter users to loyal viewers.

- Give a short description of the type of content you wish to broadcast.

- Include an image that will make your content visually appealing

- Give your channel's link to make it easy for the interested viewers to get into your stream.

- Include relevant hashtags for top ranking

- Tag relevant users like streamers, sponsors, publishers to broaden your scope.

Twitch Secrets: The Experts Guide To Become Twitch Partner

Discord

This is a free online chat website mainly for gamers. The platform allows gamers to create and join groups primarily for discussing and games and socializing. Most game streamers and publishers use this platform as a community group for their followers and subscribers. If you want to grow your channel and build a large and loyal audience, it is advisable to use discord. You can easily create categorized servers focused on topics like giveaways, general conversation, or announcements.

The platform also allows users to store videos on their servers to display their broadcast or display their stream highlights on this platform. It an ideal to maintain streamer viewer communication and foster a sense of community among the two parties. The other added advantage of this platform is that if you become consistent with steaming, your audience or fans will share your content with their friends on the forum.

Twitch Secrets: The Experts Guide To Become Twitch Partner

Online forums

Apart from promoting your Twitch channel on various social media platforms, you can also consider doing so on other online media. This can be forums, blogs, and other online communities that focus on streaming, Twitch, and any game-related topic. An excellent example of this is Reddit; Reddit has millions of active organizations devoted to Twitch gaming and streaming. If you want to attract more viewers, then don't ignore this incredible platform. Using the platform, ensure that you maintain an active presence online in those threads related to your broadcasting in general.

Do not just depend on Reddit, be active on many forums as much as you can. The more the audience you get, the more the chances of attracting more followers and viewers. Other options for your consideration include GameFAQs boards, GameSpot boards, and IGN Boards. However, keep in mind that not everyone coming to these platforms comes authentically to find twitch streams or will be interested in your streams, so do not spam them at all.

Attending Twitch cross streaming events and conventions

All you need to get as many followers as possible, and therefore you can do everything possible to achieve this. Do not just rely on your streaming social media platforms for followers; make an extra effort. Attend events like cooperative adventuring, community

Twitch Secrets: The Experts Guide To Become Twitch Partner

face-off, or Twitch con, not forgetting gaming conventions such as PAX to showcase your skills and connect with fans. When you attend these events and conventions, you will have a chance to display a stream to your audience and encourage them to follow you to your channel. You can also benefit by connecting with other streamers interested in running cross-promotional efforts like stream raiding or hosting your channel stream.

Twitch Secrets: The Experts Guide To Become Twitch Partner

How To Make A Twitch Overlay

Do you live stream on Twitch? Unless you are a mere lurker on Twitch, you're probably going to be watched when you're broadcasting. As an amateur, you may keep the Twitch account in original vanilla format. However, you will soon want to take your Twitch account to the next level with personalized stream overlays.

Fortunately, you can make Twitch overlays to match your stream's vibe, alongside your broadcasting style or whatever entertainment you are streaming. Thanks to Twitch Interactive, you can now customize your Twitch account. Using Twitch overlays, you can make something you love and repurpose graphics to create an intriguing and cohesive brand.

Although there are other options to get aesthetically pleasing overlays, serious gamers need to have an overlay that authentically reflects their gaming strength, personality, and playing style. This is what makes sense to know how to make a customized Twitch overlay.

Are you that person who is looking to beef up the visual appearance of your stream? This article will learn how to make Twitch overlay and brand your channel right from the start. Here we go.

Twitch Secrets: The Experts Guide To Become Twitch Partner

What is Twitch overlay?

Probably we're rushing too fast. Let's first hold on and look explore what is this you want to create. So, what is a Twitch Overlay?

In essence, a Twitch overlay is a design featuring a myriad of graphics that can be positioned on the video screen window while streaming to visually enhance the stream's appearance. In other words, Twitch overlays are decorations (graphical and captivating features) that augment your audience's viewing experience.

Otherwise, who would sacrifice watching a visually pleasing stream to continue watching a plain video screen? Twitch outlays brand your channel with custom designs to give it a professional look.

How to Make a Twitch overlay

The easiest way to make a custom Twitch overlay is by editing one of the many templates offered by different platforms.

You can find plenty of free yet high-quality Twitch overlays designed by experts. Interestingly, the platforms provide DIY online editors to help you fully customize the templates to match your taste.

If you fancy making Twitch overlay from scratch, you are well covered. Here are the steps to help you make your Twitch stream overlay and give your audience the best experience.

1. Open Adobe Photoshop and change the background contents to transparent. The program creates a new image measuring 1920 pixels wide and 1080 pixels tall - the visible area. You can also take a screenshot of the game you stream most and upload it as your canvas. Remember to make the screenshot a full-size image to help visualize and place overlay elements better.

Twitch Secrets: The Experts Guide To Become Twitch Partner

2. Next, start creating layers and keep things organized. You can now create one or several layers that will form the background. For multiple layers, make sure to name them to keep things organized.

3. Choose the Polygonal Tool on the left side of the menu and draw a rectangle (or desired polygon). Holding the SHIFT key when drawing shapes will help you create perfectly straight lines. Under the same menu, choose your favorite and desired background color.

4. Duplicate the layer you created, depending on the number of interactions you want to create. Merge the layers (If you want them to appear as one is on top of the other, you can duplicate the layers after merging).

5. Right-click on the layers to create a border for the banner, then customize its width and color as desired. Create a space where you will input text by dragging the layer. Be careful not to block the game screen.

6. Next, lock transparency and select desired colors for the foreground and background (Duplicate the merged layers).

7. You can add text to each polygon you created. To add text, create a new layer and use the Text Tool to label each interaction with your favorite font and color. Duplicate the layer to create a text for all interactions you intend to create.

8. Save the file in .png format. Again, remember to make the background transparent so that only your overlay parts are left in place.

Conclusion

Twitch outlay is what hooks your audience as you broadcast. With this how-to guide, you will be able to create a brilliant Twitch overlay that elevates your viewers' experience. Personalize it and give the best to your audience.

Twitch Secrets: The Experts Guide To Become Twitch Partner

How To Livestream To Twitch On A PC

Learning how to Livestream to twitch on a computer is the hottest thing to hit the internet world today. This is because there is no more need to go anywhere to catch your favorite game, movie or music being played. You can stay right at home and catch every play, game or movie that you want to. This makes your Livestream experience all the better because you don't have to waste time driving from place to place to see your favorite game or program in action.

Not only can you use your computer to Livestream to twitch on a computer, but you can also use it for other activities. Do you love playing games? If so, then you should be using your computer for that. There are tons of free online games to play, and you can even download the ones you don't own to play them.

Content form's accessibility is the driving force behind live streaming's boom on creators and consumers alike. It all takes an in a device with a screen and internet connection to twitch stream. A large number of people have access to both bodies, perfect for broadcasting. Nowadays, the bar for being a content creator is a bit higher, but it all takes more than decent streaming on a desktop computer. Here are the basics to help in a successful content creator career.

Have an idea about the content you wish to stream

Twitch Secrets: The Experts Guide To Become Twitch Partner

Twitch has recently been the only video game streaming platform but now is home to many different content types. Every content requires an extra gear. Therefore a content creator should understand this Twitch streaming for perfect streaming, not only for video games.

Gather, connect and set up your gear

It makes sense for novice broadcasters to use the lowest gears necessary for twitch streams. You can broadcast anything on your device's screen, so a webcam might not be required. Suppose you want to converse with your audience. In that case, you can prefer chatting through text chat, meaning that you don't need to look for a microphone before you commence setting up the streaming software; ensure that all essential software is correctly installed and connected. This includes even connecting the microphone and webcam to the pc because there are high chances that you might need them. Think of anything else you could wish to have, like a different screen or green screen, and get it ready.

Streaming gears

- Lighting
- Green screen
- Game capture card
- Stream deck

Install the software and connect to Twitch

Select and install that software that can work best for Twitch, for instance, OBS studio. After installing this software, it will ask for your permission on whether or not to run the automatic configuration wizard. Depending on your preferences, you might opt for a manual setup, which will get you acquainted with some essential streaming aspects. For beginners, go to file, settings, and stream in OBS Studio. Select Twitch as your service, then either connect the account to OBS studio or even decide to connect via the stream key.

Twitch Secrets: The Experts Guide To Become Twitch Partner

For the former, just login information for your twitch account. If it is the latter, get directly to Twitch, go to settings > channel and videos and copy the primary stream key you see. Paste the information on the OBS, and you will be ready to go.

Software to use on Twitch

- OBS studio - Open Broadcaster Software is a cross-platform streaming and recording application that is free and open-source, developed with Qt and maintained by the OBS Community.

- Streamlabs OBS - Streamlabs is a streaming software offering a seamless version of the interface of OBS. This genius service, designed with streamers in mind, includes a range of features to enhance your Twitch stream's visual appeal and boost viewer interaction. It also functions beyond Twitch.

- XSplit - XSplit is an application developed and maintained by SplitmediaLabs for live streaming and video-mixing. For live streaming or video recording purposes, it is often used for capturing gameplay.

- vMix - For the Windows operating system, vMix is a vision mixer program available. StudioCoast PTY LTD develops the app. It allows users to turn inputs, combine audio, record outputs, live stream cameras, video files, audio, and more in resolutions up to 4K, much like most vision mixing software.

Twitch Secrets: The Experts Guide To Become Twitch Partner

Include all video/audiovisuals and sources you intend to utilize

Everything to be broadcasted needs to be included as a source in the OBs. The game you intend to play is a source, just like the microphone and other gears, because they feed you your PC holds. If you want to show them, then ensure you add them as the source. Fortunately, when using OBS, you have an excellent opportunity to recognize the sources of your audio. If it does not show, you change it in settings, go to file, backgrounds, audio and choose the device you wish to use for audio. This implies having a device for pc audio and that for audio from the microphone.

Find the streaming settings ideal for you.

You might consider the kind of streaming settings depending on various factors like your encoder's power, type of broadcast content, and available upload bandwidth. If you need a powerful processor and higher bandwidth, then translate it to higher quality settings.

Conclusion

Are you looking for hard numbers? Twitch's guide is the perfect place to begin. From there, you will learn the essentials of twitch streams. From it, you will understand that the 720p@30fps stream requires a 3000 kbps bitrate. The latter translates to five Mbps

Twitch Secrets: The Experts Guide To Become Twitch Partner

speed. Live streaming is a rewarding experience. You can get incredible benefits if you can afford to develop streamable content from your hobby and life experiences. By making new friends, exercising your skills, or even finding new business opportunities as are far as streaming is concerned, Twitch is a perfect choice. It is the number one platform successfully opening doors and accommodating all content types ranging from ASMR, gaming, makeup tutorials, and more. The site is popular and ideal for everyone who intends to build skills in content creation.

Twitch Secrets: The Experts Guide To Become Twitch Partner

Streaming PC Specs

Unless you've been living under a rock, you might undoubtedly have heard about Twitch. This amazon owned streaming platform has over four million monthly viewers due to its vast range of streaming content ranging from gaming to model painting. Most recently, most global celebrities are the twitch streamers who reel millions of views by just spouting their opinions on specific topics or playing Fortnite. Twitch streamers have transformed their personalities into accounts that garner lucrative sponsorship deals. Twitch's pull is so intense and appealing to people like musicians, athletes, and actors who use it to stream to their audience. Creating a twitch account and starting streaming is more manageable than before. With the guide here about the streaming specs, you will make the best out of your personality on Twitch. Check out the hardware, trick, and tips for an overwhelming streaming experience.

Ideal computer for streaming

A [good computer](#) is an ideal gaming spec that is a must-have for any twitch streamer. Apart from a few exceptions, most streaming is necessitated by using a gaming desktop pc or gaming laptop. Twitch recommends that streamers use the [intel core i5-4670](#)

Twitch Secrets: The Experts Guide To Become Twitch Partner

processor, its AMD equivalent, Windows 7 or newer version, and 8GB RAM. However, those with Mac can as well stream content. Moreover, there is something that is much more important than the pc specs, guess what? An internet connection. No matter how high quality your pc specs are, they are less effective if you won't have an internet connection. You can connect through a wireless connection or prefer staying wired using ethernet for the best bitrate.

Moreover, the specs you might need will depend on the type of content to stream; if you wish to stream games, a graphic card is a must-have spec. The purpose of the card is to offer vital support to any game to be broadcasted. It would most importantly be best if you had a faster internet connection of around 3MB per second upload speed. Most home internet connections or mobile can attain this average speed. It is recommended that twitch streaming be done from a laptop but with the right specs. However, you can still decide to go the mobile way (using your phone to stream).

The resolutions you can choose from are:
- 720p @ 30fps
- 720p @ 60fps
- 1080p @ 30fps
- 1080p @ 60fps
- 2K @ 30fps
- 2K @ 60fps
- 4K @ 30fps
- 4k @ 60fps

Twitch Account

No streaming can come through without a twitch account. You first have to create a twitch account for your dreams to come true. Visit Twitch.tv for free sign-up, add a custom banner, description, and avatar to let your audience know something about you.

Twitch Secrets: The Experts Guide To Become Twitch Partner

If you want to temporarily archive your broadcasts for later viewing, go to settings, Chanel, videos, and then archive broadcasts.

Broadcasting software

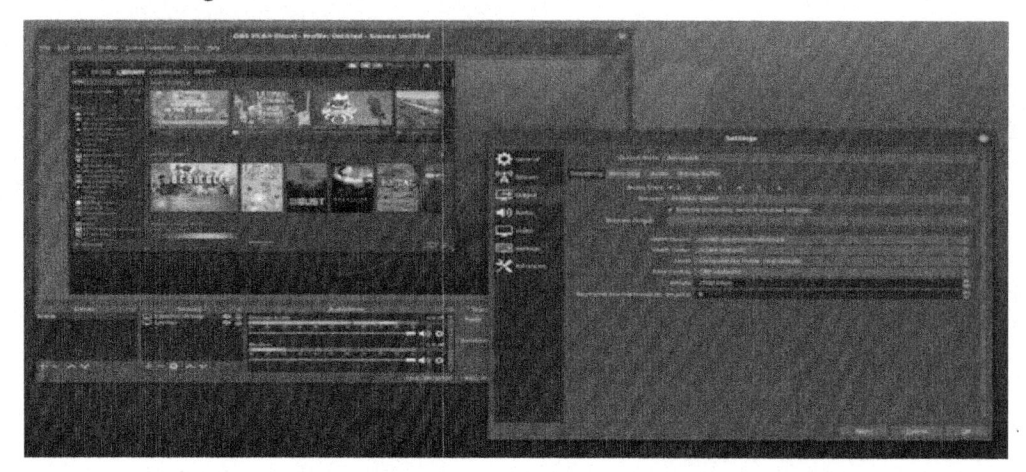

This is the most crucial part of a tool kit; streaming software shows webcams your content to audiences worldwide. The most commonly used broadcasting software is XSplit and Open Broadcasting Software (OBS). While OBS is free, XSplit contains a free tier but needs a paid subscription for you to use its critical features. Regardless of your software choice, stream software setup includes the following steps.

1. Choose your choices, for instance, computer screen, webcam, or gameplay feed.
2. Lay the sources out in a manner you want them to appear to the viewers.
3. Finally, sync up the twitch account and go live.

Besides the two major streaming software, Twitch has its broadcasting software dubbed Twitch Studio. This studio is currently available in beta and is designed to be an all-in-one broadcasting just like XSplit and OBS . the platform allows users to create several scenes with different audio and video sources and packs in various on-screen and inbuilt notification options.

Twitch Secrets: The Experts Guide To Become Twitch Partner

Good Quality Equipment

Although you can stream using a gaming headset, a quality microphone that will allow your viewers to get what you say clearly is essential. There are several microphones in the market today, most of which whose effectiveness and quality are questionable. Bit Yeti USB mic that goes one hundred and twenty-nine dollars is the best to assure you much clarity. Thanks to its adjustable pickup modes and crisp audio quality. However, people have different needs and budgets; what might work for you might not for another. Consider the thirty-six-dollar Samson go mic if you have a tight budget. Moreover, if you need a more lightweight and portable mic, you can consider Blue Yeti Nano, which goes at ninety-nine dollars.

Besides a good microphone, you also need the best cameras or webcam to ensure that your viewers see you. One of the best webcam for your consideration is the Logitech pro c920, which features a wide field of view and 1080p capture quality. If you prefer some higher-end webcam, then go for the Logitech Stream Cam that offers 60 fps and 1080p capture while touting the capacity to work in portrait orientation for mobile-friendly videos.

Here are a few basic items to get you started:

Mpow Gaming Headset: https://amzn.to/3a2fDCb

Twitch Secrets: The Experts Guide To Become Twitch Partner

Blue Yeti USB Mic for Recording & Streaming: https://amzn.to/3cSWd4J

Twitch Secrets: The Experts Guide To Become Twitch Partner

Neewer Ring Light Kit:1 8": https://amzn.to/2LElJj0

Elgato Green Screen: https://amzn.to/2MT5kaR

Twitch Secrets: The Experts Guide To Become Twitch Partner

Logitech C920 Hd Pro Webcam (Black): https://amzn.to/3q5dyv1

Twitch Secrets: The Experts Guide To Become Twitch Partner

Corsair K55 RGB Gaming Keyboard: https://amzn.to/3oZrzJi

Benvo Extended Mouse Pad: https://amzn.to/3a6JsBT

Twitch Secrets: The Experts Guide To Become Twitch Partner

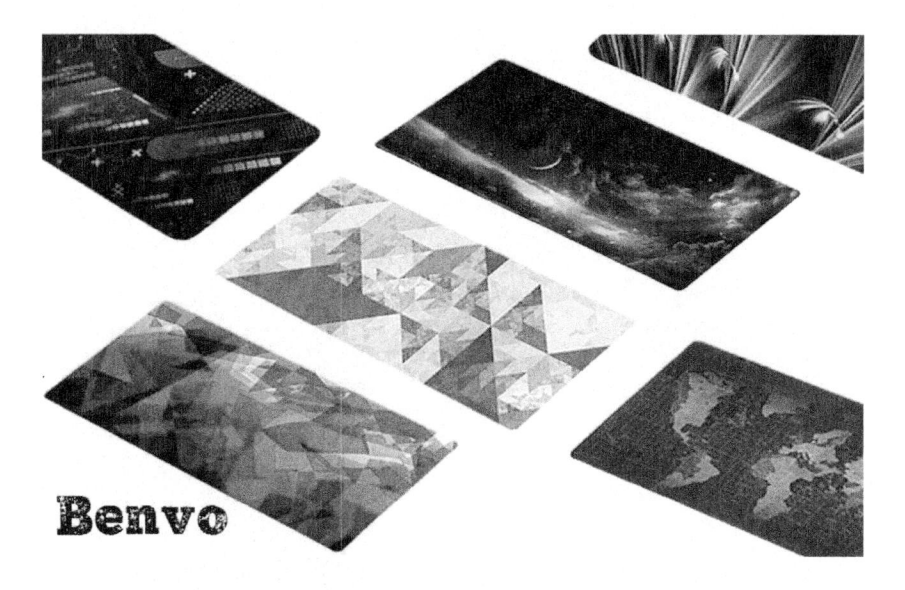

Govee 65.6ft Alexa LED Strip Lights: https://amzn.to/2MT7HKN

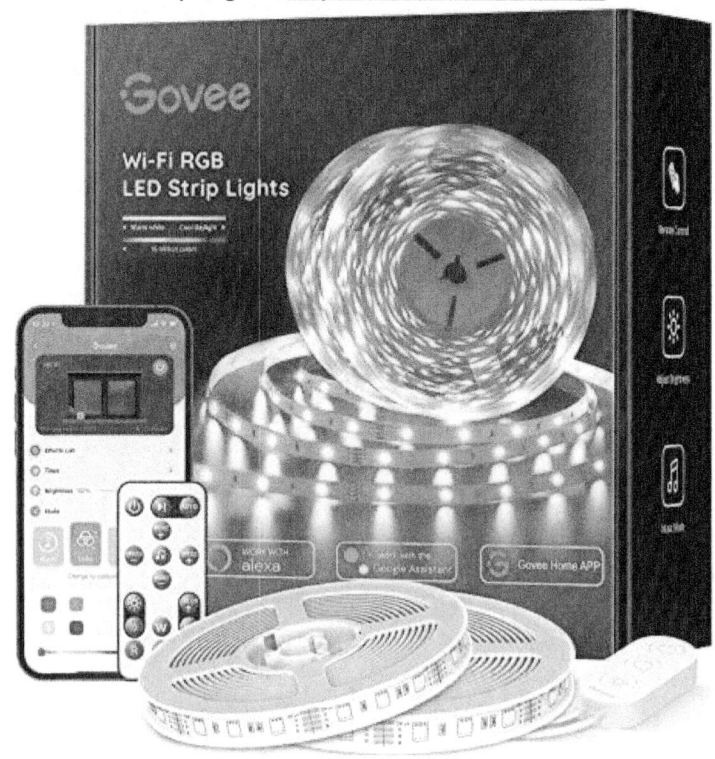

Logitech G502 Hero High Performance Gaming Mouse: https://amzn.to/2MPqhUe

Twitch Secrets: The Experts Guide To Become Twitch Partner

Okeysen Gaming Chair: https://amzn.to/3jzWx9Z

Twitch Secrets: The Experts Guide To Become Twitch Partner

The Difference Between Twitch Streaming Vs. YouTube Streaming

Getting into the streaming industry requires a perfect platform to air your videos. The two primary options for personal projects and livestreaming are YouTube and twitch—these two platforms almost similar in functionality but have some critical differences that might interfere with your choice. Here are essential features for the two platforms to help you make a sound decision.

General findings

- Youtube allows for general live streaming; in other words, you can stream what you wish to, while Twitch only focuses on gaming, although there are different streaming categories available.

- Youtube exists alongside the content your channel produces, while on Twitch, the only content on your channel relates to streaming.

- Youtube helps its users to make money from ads, memberships, and super chats, while Twitch allows account holders to earn from ads, subscriptions, Bits, ads, and direct donations.

Twitch Secrets: The Experts Guide To Become Twitch Partner

- Youtube is free to use, and the status of the user affects monetization. Twitch is also to use, but some features are locked behind partner or affiliate status.

The platform you select will depend on your streaming goals. These two platforms are almost equal choices for newbies in the streaming field. However, if you have created a youtube channel, it will be better to stick to it and build on your existing audience rather than start over again on Twitch. Both platforms offer excellent opportunities for people to make money from their streams. In most instances, the features on these platforms involve sharing a portion with the platform developer. For those who have Twitch, accounts have an added advantage because Twitch includes direct donations that allow the users to keep the money donated by their viewers.

Content creation: YouTube has more variety

In terms of content creation, YouTube has more variety compared to Twitch. YouTube contains streams and more produced content, while Twitch has streams, archived videos, and clips.

YouTube makes a perfect choice for those users who are not only interested in streaming. Apart from just uploading stream recordings to your channel, YouTube allows for uploading previously polished videos to help attract more viewers to the track.

On Twitch, the audience depends on how viewers are interested in your stream, not the YouTube case. There, you can build an audience from non-live content and attract more people when you do.

Discover: Twitch is more user-friendly, and youtube is user-friendly.

- The search results cover every content on youtube, whether it is life or not, while on Twitch, search results depend on game topics and titles.

Twitch Secrets: The Experts Guide To Become Twitch Partner

- Youtube channel subscribers can easily find your stream, while Twitch is themed mostly on gaming.

- If you are a viewer looking for some content to watch, Twitch is much easier for you than youtube. It allows channel visitors to search by a specific game title and get notifications whenever a live stream commences. However, this requires the viewer to go to the stream's detailed URL and click a button to get the message.

On the side of the streamer, youtube has an edge. Since Twitch is game-focused, the platform does not have the structure perfect for other content types. Although the system has included different categories like IRL, music, and creative, the classes are not specific to the game title system's initial area. This means that your viewers might not find your channel if you are not streaming a game. Youtube users are used to every content type, so the search function plays a vital role.

Twitch channel archives recordings for fourteen days for primary users, so if you can't download the content by then, the system will delete it. A user can only extend this grace period to sixty days by earning the partner status. Twitch has other premium features like custom emotes for polls, priority customer service, and chat.

On youtube, the Livestream recording goes directly to the user's channel immediately after broadcasting, and you can stay there without necessarily doing anything. You have to join youtube's partner program to earn money from your channel, but besides that, all users have access to similar features.

Monetization

On monetization, Twitch has a slight advantage over youtube because of its donations. Youtube users can make money from super chats, ads, and memberships, while twitch users can earn money from direct donations. Both Twitch and youtube take some commissions from most user income. To gain from Youtube, you need a youtube partner status while Twitch needs either a partner or affiliate status.

Twitch Secrets: The Experts Guide To Become Twitch Partner

Regardless of the site you decide to use, official forms of monetization like chat-based rewards and ads require a certain level of popularity. For instance, to access Twitch account referral programs, the streamer must have at least fifty followers in a month, have streamed for over five hundred minutes in at least seven different days while maintaining at least three concurrent visitors. For one to achieve the partner status, the requirements are elevated even more.

Twitch Secrets: The Experts Guide To Become Twitch Partner

What Type Of Content Creator Do You Want To Be For Streaming On Twitch

Today, most twitch stream viewers use what type of content creator do you want to be for streaming on Twitch. The majority of people who stream on Twitch are using what type of content creator do you want to be. While some stream viewers still use the old "fancy" viewer programs, the vast majority of them are using the programs that are built specifically for streaming. When it comes to streaming, you want your stream viewer to have the ability to have everything they need available at their fingertips.

If you want to earn a living online and become a successful streaming game host, you need to start thinking about what type of content creator you want to be? This is one of the first decisions you need to make to start streaming on Twitch. You have a lot of choices. There are hundreds to thousands of different programs available. Which one will work best for you?

What type of content creator do you want to be? There are many types of programs that allow you to stream video games. Some of them are better than others. Some of the options you have to include:

Know your interest

Twitch Secrets: The Experts Guide To Become Twitch Partner

What type of game are you interested in playing? If you like to play many different kinds of games, you might want to create a program that streams all kinds of them. This way you can enjoy them whenever you want and wherever you are. However, if you have a particular game or genre of game that you like to play, it is important to find a program that will work. This will help you stream longer and enjoy the game more.

Do you want to broadcast yourself on Twitch live? This is something that some people find very enjoyable. To do this, you need to find a program that allows you to stream yourself. This will be much easier if you want to advertise yourself or find someone to stream for you.

Start a date

Once you have decided what type of content creator you want to be for streaming on Twitch, start searching for it. There are some different places to look for one, such as Google docs or forums. You may also want to look online for what type of content creator you want to be for streaming on Twitch.

Once the platform is set up and running, you can start broadcasting your streams live to your followers. Most platforms that offer streaming will give you the option of either having your stream be direct or indirect. If you plan to stream on Twitch from your website or blog, then the direct option will probably be best for you. This means that anyone who clicks on your twitch stream will be able to see your site or blog directly. For websites or blogs, this is not recommended. Direct streaming means that anyone who clicks on your twitch stream will be able to go now to your site or blog, where they can find any information they want.

Aim your one year goals

Setting your objectives also gives you a great place to start when you're starting. By having something written down where you can see it every day, you'll be less likely to stray from your goal. You want to become a successful streamer, but sometimes you can't know what to do or where to start without having your goal in front of you.

Twitch Secrets: The Experts Guide To Become Twitch Partner

Also, you can use your objective as a jumping-off point. If you fail at your objective, then you know what you didn't do enough. This will help you avoid repeating your mistakes. Also, it will help you gain perspective. This is very important if you want to become the best or even the ultimate master streamer.

You can only be one person. Even if you have a million followers and you think you can be the best of them all, you're still one person. So don't set lofty goals for yourself. Instead, set smaller goals for each day to help keep you motivated!

By having these one-year goals, you'll keep yourself focused and motivated. And you will succeed, regardless of your brand new or have been doing this game for a while. Remember, this game doesn't make you rich. It makes you healthier and more focused! You deserve it! Go for it!

Have an inspiration

The best way to get a streaming viewership that will help you make a lot of money is to act like the big dogs, and the best way to do that is to emulate 3 to 5 content creators. You want to be able to attract attention and have people want to come to watch your stream. This is one way to draw in the traffic you need for your site or your twitch channel.

The simplest goal is, of course, to become the best. But it's not always that easy. Sometimes you have to work for it. If you're doing well, for now, you have to work even harder to get to the next level. Don't set yourself up for failure. Instead, be positive and have fun!

Twitch Secrets: The Experts Guide To Become Twitch Partner

Best Free Twitch Overlay To Use For Your Streams

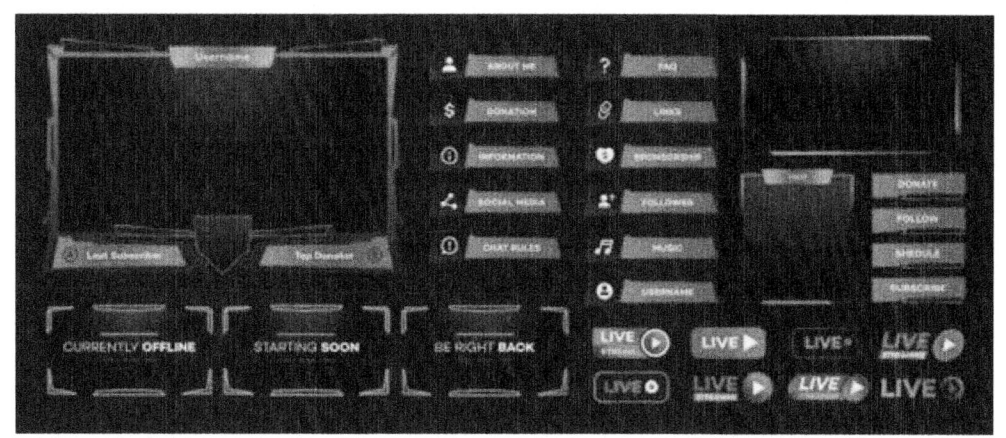

Visual appeal plays a huge role in attracting an audience when streaming for Twitch. This helps you create and build your brand and help your audience associate the brand to the person.

For new streamers, chances are they stick to the normal, boring, old format on the screen. That's completely understandable for someone who is just starting and feeling things through. But, once streamers have built their platform and their brand, they usually opt to add more personal touches to their stream formats.

Typically, we see these personalized stream formats on how they design the layout of what is seen on screen. Overlays are used to add personality or incorporate one's style to their display. An overlay is a 1080p resolution border placed around the picture captured by your webcam or the captured window of your display.

When choosing the type of overlay you want for your channel, it falls on personal preferences. The design has to reflect who and what you are as a person and resonate with the brand that you have built. Remember, when building a brand that caters to your fans, you want it to be as dynamic and sincere as possible.

Twitch Secrets: The Experts Guide To Become Twitch Partner

In building your brand and expressing yourself through your layout, you have to find a good designer that truly caters to your needs and delivers the best quality of work out there. You don't have to break the bank to achieve what you want for your overlay. Some sites offer great deals for Twitch overlays. Here are a few of the best free Twitch Overlays to use for your streams!

OWN3D Overlay Packs

Own3D offers a wide assortment of high-quality designs that features Free and Premium membership, static and animated designs, webcam overlays and talking screens. Own3D prides itself on providing quality at a reasonable rate for streamers. The complete package offers both static and animated screens, overlays and graphics. Their site is easy to navigate. Just look up the style or color you prefer to find a package that best suits your liking.

If you're keen on looking for overlays, then you have to check out Own3D's vast collection. Many of those offered on their site allow you to add your socials and other information specific to your stream. Own3D works with qualified designers whose goal is to create designs to help your streams look more engaging and visually pleasing.

Own3D packs are compatible with major streaming sites like Twitch, YouTube Gaming and Facebook Gaming. They're also compatible with OBS, Streamlabs OBS, and StreamElements.

On Own3D, there are multitudes of free stream templates and graphic packages you can get your hands on. Many streamers opt for the more minimalistic approach or are designed for a specific game in mind. Some free designs are customizable; you could incorporate your social media and other details into the design seamlessly. These could also be edited with Adobe, GIMP or any other design software.

Twitch Secrets: The Experts Guide To Become Twitch Partner

Nerd or Die Twitch Overlays

Nerd or Die has truly marked itself as one of the best service providers for stream graphic design. One great perk that Nerd or Die offers apart from their designs is the other free resources they have, like their free tool that allows streamers to make panels that would cater to the needs of their brands.

Nerd or Die originally started as a tutorial website and YouTube Channel but has evolved into a brand that produces products for live streaming designs and tutorials for consumers worldwide.

Twitch Secrets: The Experts Guide To Become Twitch Partner

Although Nerd or Die's overlays were initially designed for Twitch, almost all of their designs work well with Facebook, YouTube Gaming, Mixer and a whole lot more.

Currently, Nerd or Die offers around 40 different packages that include overlays in their design. Apart from being compatible with streaming services, they are also compatible with OBS, Streamlabs OBS and XSplit. In addition to this, they are fully supported with StreamLabs and StreamElements.

A great feature that Nerd or Die's shop features are showing some of their products at a suggested price. With these, you can adjust the price to however much you feel comfortable paying (even if it's nothing at all), but some packages are marketed as free.

Placeit - Twitch Overlay Maker

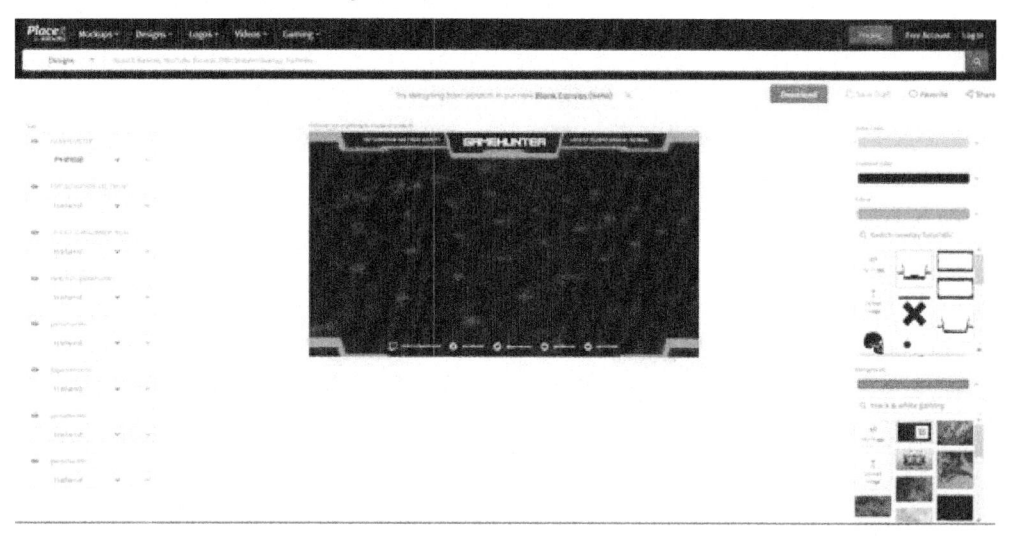

Placeit is an online design maker that offers easy-to-use tools to create professional-looking overlays and banners that will make you stand out from the rest on Twitch, YouTube, and other social media sites. They also offer video and realistic mockups.

Placeit offers hundreds of Twitch design templates that are fully customizable and are made to fit the current formats and sizes. Placeit has Fast Preview for video content - a feature you can use to view the progress and changes live while you're editing.

Twitch Secrets: The Experts Guide To Become Twitch Partner

Gamers can choose from various options, including OBS Streams Overlay Maker, Social Media Cover, Twitch Banner Maker, Twitch Offline Banner Maker, Twitch Overlay Maker, Twitch Panel Maker, and Webcam Frame.

Using Placeit is easy. Once you've chosen your style, customized and finished your template, all you have to do is download and get the vector version of it. If you need to work on it again, you could just go back to your previous downloads.

Streamlabs Prime Overlays

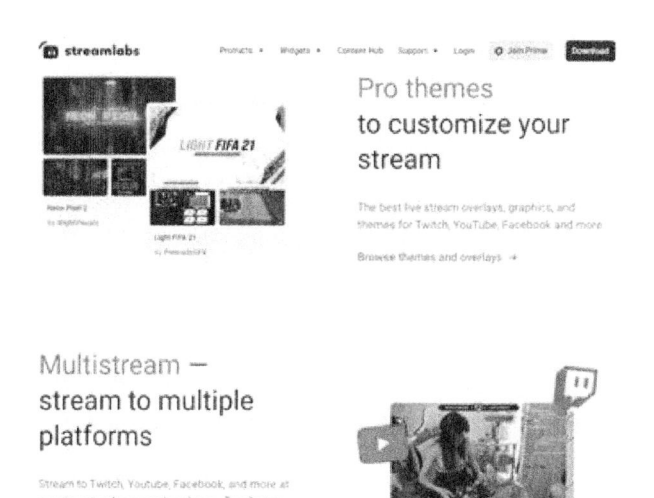

If you're using Streamlabs OBS or the Streamlabs cloud bot, you may be aware of Streamlabs Prime: the platform's premium service. Although Streamlabs Prime costs a monthly fee, it offers many benefits that could help streamers grow and monetize their streams.

Streamlabs Prime leases popular overlays from other third-party companies. This allows their users to switch up their looks whenever they want. Apart from this, Streamlabs Prime offers other benefits such as including greater margins on your merch for your stream, better internet options for IRL streams and widgets that generate engagement.

Twitch Secrets: The Experts Guide To Become Twitch Partner

Visuals By Impulse Overlay Designs

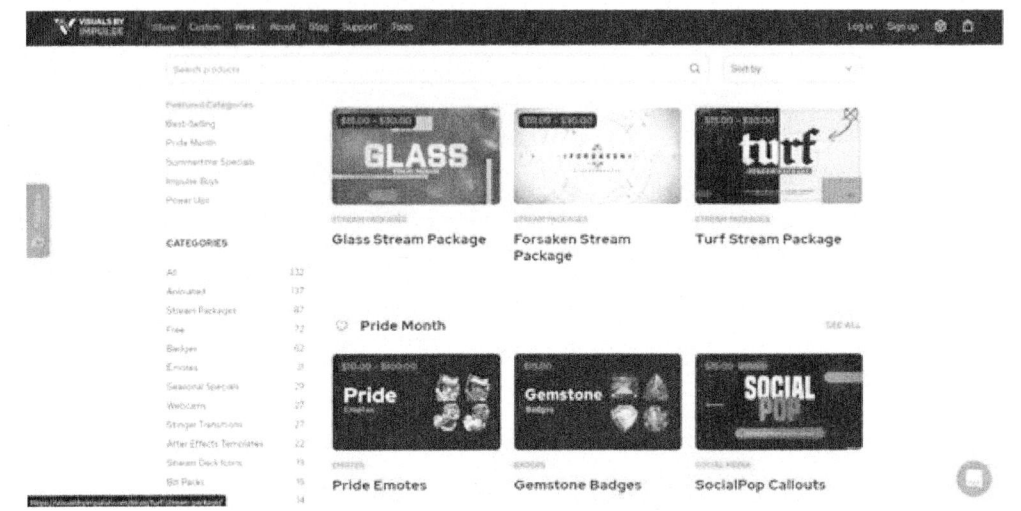

Visuals by Impulse offers a wide array of graphic designs that can be purchased individually or in a package. This site was created by a fellow streamer named Caleb, who wanted to offer other broadcasters free and affordable graphics for their channels. Caleb and his team enjoys seeing and watching other streamers develop their various offer brands and styles into something more special and eccentric.

Visuals by Impulse's products are either pre-made or custom-designed graphics. Their designs showcase both static and animated variations, both of which are for brandable images.

Their designs are compatible with major streaming platforms like Twitch, Youtube Gaming, Facebook Gaming, etc. Their graphics are compatible with OBS, Streamlabs OBS, Lightstream, XSplit and others.

Twitch Secrets: The Experts Guide To Become Twitch Partner

StreamShark Graphics

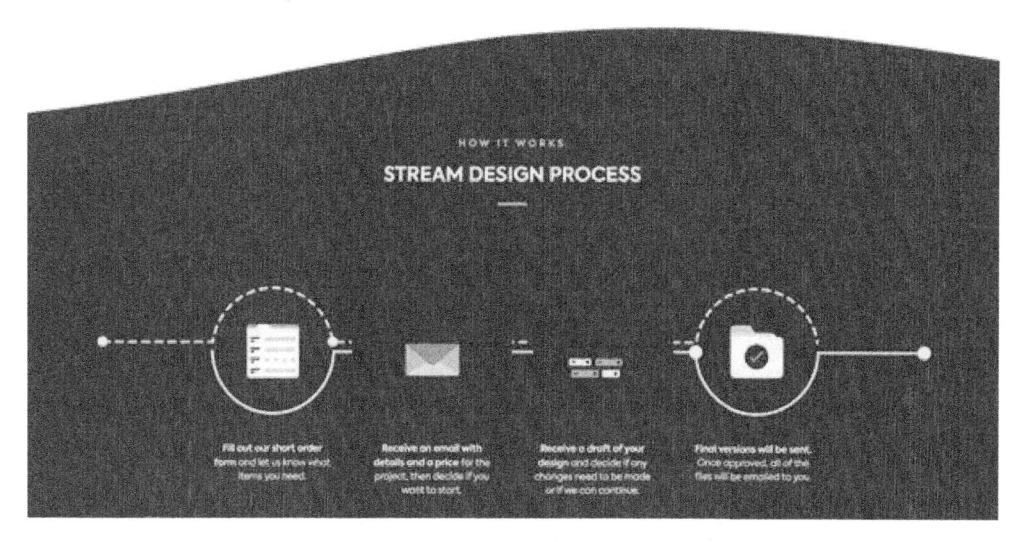

StreamShark Graphics is a one-stop shop for all your streaming design needs. They are a group of designers who make custom, personalized graphics for Twitch Channels. StreamShark can create overlays, panels and can, from various offers, create gaming logos. They are known for their illustration, design and animation.

Ghost Rising - Twitch Overlay

Twitch Secrets: The Experts Guide To Become Twitch Partner

Just like its name suggests, Ghost Rising - Twitch Overlay specializes in overlays for Twitch live streaming. Although, don't let the name fool you, as it offers the same high-quality designs for other streaming sites like YouTube, Beam and the like. They have a wide array of custom stream designs for anyone who wants something more custom.

They offer over a dozen Twitch overlays, free profile graphics, stream screens, Twitch Alert, and a full stream package. But, if you're willing to spend somewhere between $2 and $26, they offer premium downloads, which include overlays.

Twitch Secrets: The Experts Guide To Become Twitch Partner

Best Green Screens for Streamers

Green screens enable you to create new scenes and edit in special effects to your Twitch streams or YouTube videos. Green screens are relatively cheap and easy to set up with broadcasting softwares such as OBS and streamlabs. In addition to this, green screens give you the option of removing your background and replacing it, creating new scenes for your viewers.

Green screens work by providing a solid color that can easily be manipulated with a chroma key editor. These could be set up with software to remove the background or replace the green with another image or video. Popular streamers and YouTubers make use of this to enhance the viewing experience of their audience. A good example of this is how Pewdiepie uses a greenscreen when streaming games to visualize the game fuller. A rectangle at the bottom or top of a screen takes up space from a game's visuals when rolled inches in the green screen. Therefore, cutting corners (literally) helps make the game visuals more visible without sacrificing the reaction camera of the streamer while streaming. It gives a cleaner look altogether.

For those who don't want to spend money on a green screen, you could use anything that is one solid color, and that is wide and tall enough to give your background coverage in replacement for a green screen. You could paint your wall, use a solid-coloured blanket, tub, or anything that is relatively smooth. It's best to consider using things that absorb light to make it

Twitch Secrets: The Experts Guide To Become Twitch Partner

cleaner. In addition to this, if you end up using a cloth (like a blanket), consider running a steamer through it to remove the crumples and fold lines off it to give it a smoother look.

On the other hand, if you choose to invest in a green screen, the price range is around $40 to $250. This is completely dependent on the size, quality and brand. Here's a list of green screens that have been tried, tested and recommended by streamers:

Webaround Big Shot Cair Green Screen

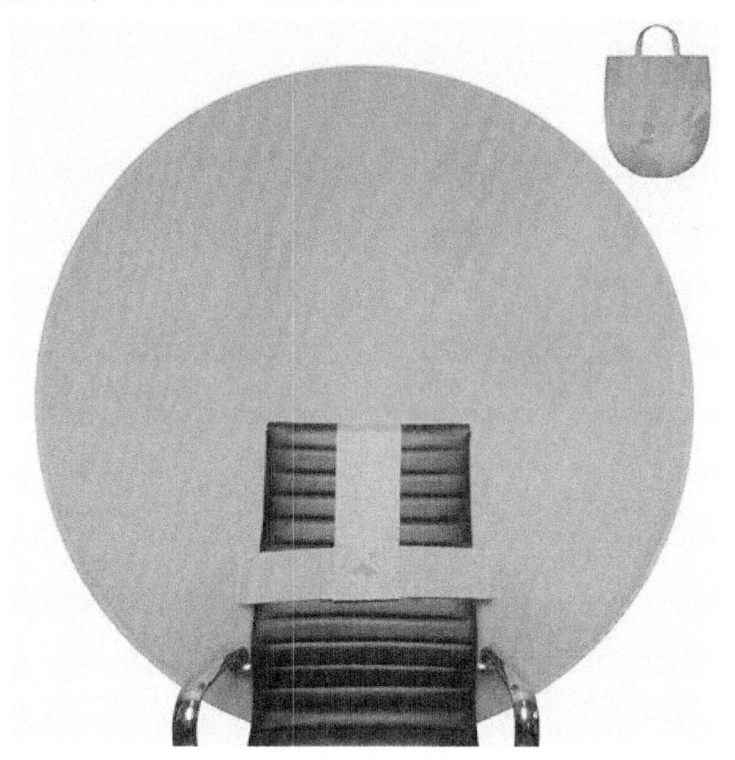

Webaround offers green screens that attach themselves to the back of chairs. This gives people access to small spaces to chroma key technology without sacrificing too much space. The company was founded by Linda Bovay, who saw that people needed a portable green screen that was compact and easy to set up and put away.

The best thing about this is that it attaches itself to your gaming chair. With this, you don't have to ensure that it has to rest on something behind it to stay stable. This is very easy to unpack

Twitch Secrets: The Experts Guide To Become Twitch Partner

and put away. Therefore you shouldn't have to worry about setting up and cleaning up before and after your streams.

The only downside with this is that with the green screen being so close, you will have to ensure that your chair stays in position and that your lighting stays on track. Despite this, many streamers use this product and end up with excellent-quality streams.

Aside from the green screen itself, it comes with a tote bag for easy storage and transport. The Webaround brand offers more products, but we strongly suggest you go for the Big Shot to give you the most coverage. This green screen is 56" in diameter and comes in both green and gray.

FotoDiox Collapsible 2-Sided Chroma-Key Panel

This collapsible chroma-key panel is double-sided with two different colors (as seen in the photo above), allowing you to decide whether you want to go with the green or blue screen. Having two different colors on a chroma-key panel enables you with flexibility in what you can wear and show on-stream. The thing with green screens is you can't wear or show anything green while you're in front of a green screen because the software will read that green color as your background despite it being something you want to showcase.

This 5 x 7 green screen isn't necessarily the largest green screen out there, but many lighting is slightly happy while using it for their streams or taking photographs that they use for graphics. The screen also comes with a collapsible stand that makes things easier for storage.

Twitch Secrets: The Experts Guide To Become Twitch Partner

Setting up the Fotodiox collapsible panel can be easily done in less than two minutes. And, when it's packed up, it barely takes up much space, so this is great for streamers who have a narrow gap behind them while streaming.

Elgato Collapsible Green Screen

Arguably one of the best collapsible green screens ever made, the Elgato collapsible green screen is a high-quality product that truly suits high-quality video production. The green screen fabric is dust and wrinkle-resistant, thus making it an extra-reliable choice for streaming.

The screen boasts its set-up record of 3 seconds, being lifted at a suitable height. The Elgato measures at 61.02" x 72.44" inches when it is fully open, which gives you ample space to place behind your desk while streaming. The aluminum frame ensures that the chroma key stays in perfect condition without causing any unwanted shadows in your video output throughout your stream.

The green screen rolls up and down into a hard case that easily fits small spaces. You can easily store this under a long desk, a closet, under your bed and in the trunk of your car. The Elgato measures at 3.94" x 4.72" x 61.02" inches when the green screen is rolled in.

On top of the excellent quality that this already boasts, Elgato offers a 1-year warranty with their product to ensure that any manufacturing errors are replaced and have 100% customer satisfaction.

Twitch Secrets: The Experts Guide To Become Twitch Partner

Fancierstudio Chromakey Green Screen Kit

If you've got more space around your streaming area, then the Fancierstudio Green Screen Kit might be the best option for you! The kit includes a 10' x 12' green screen backdrop made when the green screen is rolled in. Therefore creating inches enables fabric, an 8' x 10' aluminum support to hold up the green screen, two 33" umbrella light stands and a carrying case. Take note, and these 105-watt CFL bumps are not included in the kit.

This is relatively simple to set up and adjust. Given that it has a travelling caseThe leaning up and travelling with the kit is much simpler. One downside of this is having to learn how to remove all the wrinkles from the green screen from time to time and meticulously angle the lights to ensure no shadows. Also, it is advisable to place the stands of the green screen against the wall to add stability to them.

The larger background means you have more free reign over the activities you could do for your streams, as you have more room while in front of your camera.

Twitch Secrets: The Experts Guide To Become Twitch Partner

Linco Studio Kit

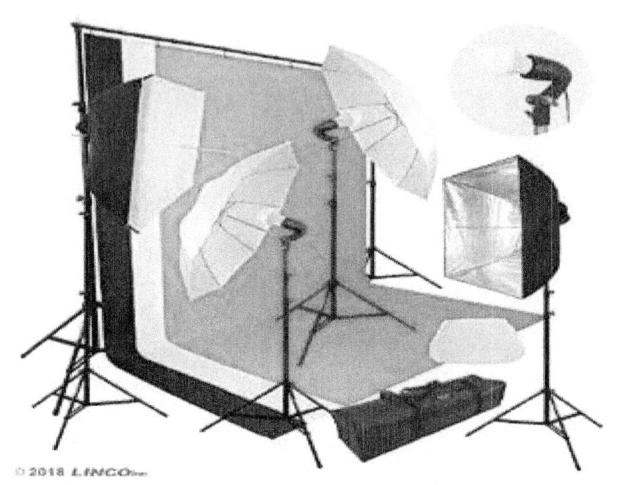

The Linco Photo Studio lighting kit is the choice for you if you want to have a big chroma key background with multiple colors to choose from. This kit comes with three Muslim backdrops in green, black, and white, a green screen stand, a full lighting system, studio clips and a caring case.

This is such a great kit for content creators who have a small space but need a green screen to use for the content they're shooting while standing up. The backdrops are 5' x 10' feet in measure and are washable. The Muslim clothes are very durable, and they absorb light instead of reflecting it.

Twitch Secrets: The Experts Guide To Become Twitch Partner

Best Lighting for Streaming

Lighting plays a very important role in the video output quality of your stream. This plays a vital role in the brightness and darkness of your frame and adds to the video output's overall tone, mood, and atmosphere. With this, it is very important to control the lighting in your space to get the best texture, vibrancy of color, and luminosity on what you're putting in focus. There is a certain art to distributing the shadows and highlights to your frame to obtain a professional-looking setup, and it's best achieved with the right equipment.

Being a new streamer, you don't have to deck out on the most expensive and state-of-the-art equipment out there. It's best to use what you have or purchase the piece of equipment within your means. What kind of lighting you need depends on what you already have and want to add. To understand this further, here's a more in-depth and technical guide to the basics of lighting.

The Lighting Basics

Starting with your streaming setup requires time to build up to. It would be advisable to add one piece of equipment at a time instead of buying it all in one go. Also, it is notable that even if you get the most expensive piece of lighting equipment, it might not work out for you if you're using it wrong. There are different types of lighting equipment that serve different purposes. There's the main three:

Twitch Secrets: The Experts Guide To Become Twitch Partner

1. **Key Light** - this is the primary source of light that you must have in front of you. This is traditionally placed at a 45-degree angle to your camera, slightly above and tilted down towards you.

2. **Fill Light** - this is a supplementary light to your key light. This is typically placed beside the key light to cancel out any shadows that the key light might have formed. This also helps you stand out more in-camera. With the lessened appearance of shadows, you are indeed to look more radiant and well-put-together.

3. **Back Light** - This light source generally separates the camera's main focus from its background. This adds a more obvious separation between you and your background, making you pop out more on-screen.

Best lights for game streamers:

Aputure Amaran HR672s

The Aputure Amaran HR672S light is great at casting an even white light, making it a great key light for your setup. This has a CRI of 95+, which means that the light this produces looks very natural and that it falls where it needs to fall. In other words, it's very flattering. In addition to this,

Twitch Secrets: The Experts Guide To Become Twitch Partner

the Aputure Amaran HR672S has eco-friendly bulbs that are built to last, boasting a mega 100,000 hours of bright lights!

Mobility is not an issue with the Aputure Amaran HR672S, as you can take these lights with you anywhere. These come with an AC adaptor for indoor use, but this product can also be battery-powered. Just plug in lithium batteries, and you're good to go! Not to mention that the lights are completely adjustable, as you could set the perfect ISO for your surroundings to fully encapsulate the feel and tone that you're going for.

Aside from the lights themselves, the [Aputure Amaran HR672S](#) also comes with a wireless remote, a lamp bracket, an adapter, an orange filter and more!

Elgato Key Light

HIGH-END STUDIO LIGHTING
Quality lighting is the secret to making your camera feed shine.

PREMIUM LEDS
160 OSRAM LEDs

ULTRA-BRIGHT AND DIMMABLE
2800 lumens

VERSATILE COLOR TEMPERATURE
2900 – 7000 K

SILKY-SMOOTH OPAL GLASS
Guarantees balanced, glare-free diffusion

OSRAM
LED Included

Elgato is a brand that is widely known for creating products that cater well with streamers. The Elgato Key Light is no exception to this, as this comes with a very flexible stand that mounts directly on your desk. The height of the light can be raised or lowered, and the general direction

Twitch Secrets: The Experts Guide To Become Twitch Partner

of the light can be tilted or rotated to get the perfect angle you need for your streams. The flexibility enables you to simply add the light in the current setup to your room lightning enable when the green screen is rolled in, moving bits and bobs around to make things and the positioning work.

One major factor as to why this key light is best for streaming is that it doesn't give off much heat, considering the brightness it produces. The color temperature of this light ranges from 2900 to 7000K (which can be adjusted in the downloadable application on your PC), but it doesn't radiate as much heat compared to other lights with the same function. This is a great point to consider since streaming rooms can be quite hot due to many factors, and lighting is one major factor for the heat.

Emart 60 LED

The Emart 60 LED lighting kit comes in a set of two lights that can easily be placed on top of your desk or table. The lights are set at a balanced 550K and provide 15W LED continuous lighting. The Emart 60 LED lighting kit is typically used to photograph items, but these also work as a great key and fill light for your setup if it is positioned close to your body.

As aforementioned, the kit comes with two lights that are powered via an AC/DC adapter. The lights can be tilted up to 180-degrees. The kit also comes with four different color filters, which you can use to add flare to your streams. Also, each light comes with its stand.

Twitch Secrets: The Experts Guide To Become Twitch Partner

Although these pale compared to the two products listed above, this is great starter equipment to teach yourself where and how to position your lights in your setup. The Emart 60 LED light kit is very much budget and beginner-friendly, which is very suitable for small creators who need the added lighting to their setups.

Neewer Ring

The Neewer ring light is as high quality as it is versatile. Coming with 18-inch diameter, the ring light is fully dimmable, which allows you to choose a certain brightness for the vibe of your stream. The ring light is built with an impressive 240 LED bulbs that make up the ring, which promises the best results a ring light could ever deliver.

Apart from the lights themselves, the kit comes with an aluminum-alloy stand with a maximum height of 61-inches. It also includes a ball head adapter that allows you to put a device onto the center of the ring light to maximize its effects. A carrying case and two color filters (white and orange) are also included in the kit.

Twitch Secrets: The Experts Guide To Become Twitch Partner

The Crenova Ring Light

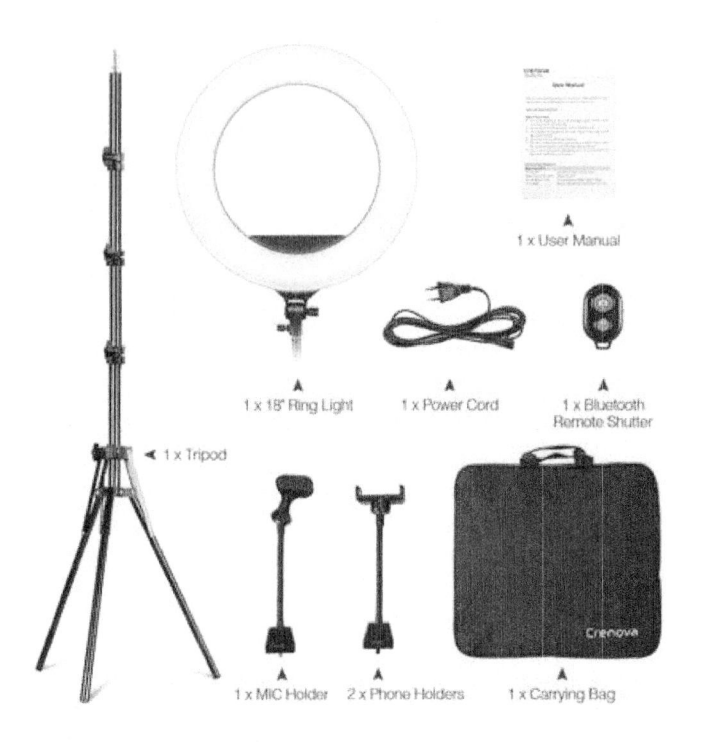

The Crenova Ring Light is the best ring light to trot around with for your IRL streams. This has a 10-inch diameter with 120 LED bulbs, completely adjustable with ten different brightness settings. With this, you're sure to look rather dashing at all your streams!

The tripod attachment allows the ring light to be sat prettily on your desk, and, with its low center of gravity due to its height, it promises nothing but stability for your lighting. But, if you need a taller tripod in the future, this is completely replaceable. The Crenova Ring Light is completely flexible, boasting a 360-degree rotation that gives you the perfect angle.

As mentioned earlier, this is the best ring light for IRL streaming since it's lightweight and since you can simply attach your mobile phone to the center of the ring. Stop no matter what angle you face or how dark or unflattering the room's lighting is. Your lighting always carries a very flattering source of light with you, right in front of your camera!

Twitch Secrets: The Experts Guide To Become Twitch Partner

Nanoleaf Light Panels

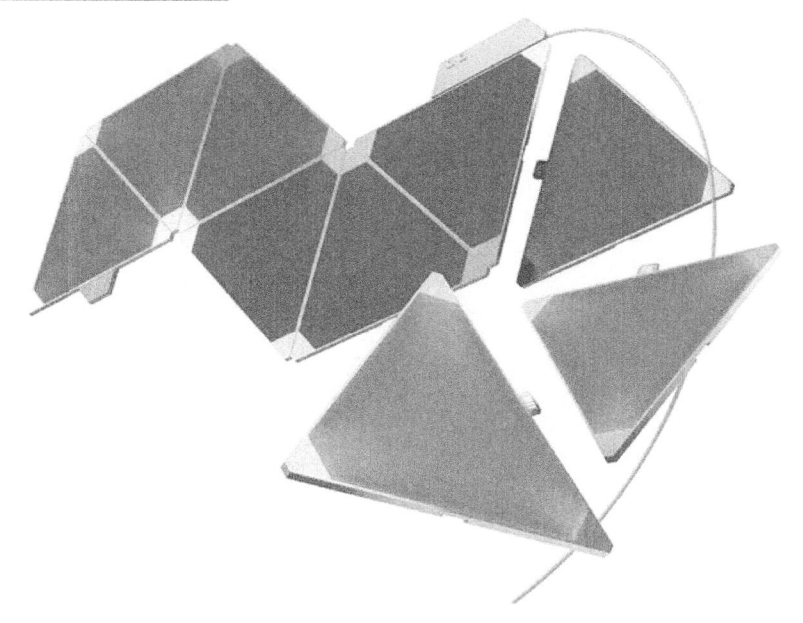

The Nanoleaf Light Panels are completely creative, customizable background lights that can be set to your brand's colour or changed regularly depending on the kind of content you'll be making for the stream. The high-tech lights can be controlled through voice-command, their app or the remote control that comes with the kit or integrated with their integration hub (Amazon Alexa or Google Assistant).

Let your creativity shine and take control while setting up the Nanoleaf Light Panels. Each panel can be manually placed piece by piece to form a design that coincides with your aesthetics or blends with its environment. Nanoleaf Light Panels offer a cool feature for synchronizing the lights with the music you're playing, which helps build a subtle yet eye-catching experience for your viewers.

Each light can be set to one of 16 million colors available, but it also comes with preset color options if you just want something that already looks nice. To top it all off, you could even set the colors to change at certain times throughout the day or throughout your stream for added (natural-looking) effects!

Twitch Secrets: The Experts Guide To Become Twitch Partner

Philips Hue 2m Strip Light

No gamer or streaming room is complete without the strip lights going around the room or the table. It has become such a staple aesthetic for streamers and gamers alike. It must be something about keeping the RGB aesthetic of their hardware cohesive with their rooms.

The Philips Hue 2m Strip Light is easy to install on any surface that you choose. The strip lights come with many features that highlight the user's interest and the product itself's functionality. These include easy dimming, smart control, and lighting must-creating. Therefore room's Stopillion colors to choose from and timers. All of which you can control through voice command or simply having it light up as you enter your home.

Twitch Secrets: The Experts Guide To Become Twitch Partner

Best Twitch Panels to Use For Your Streams and Where to Get Them

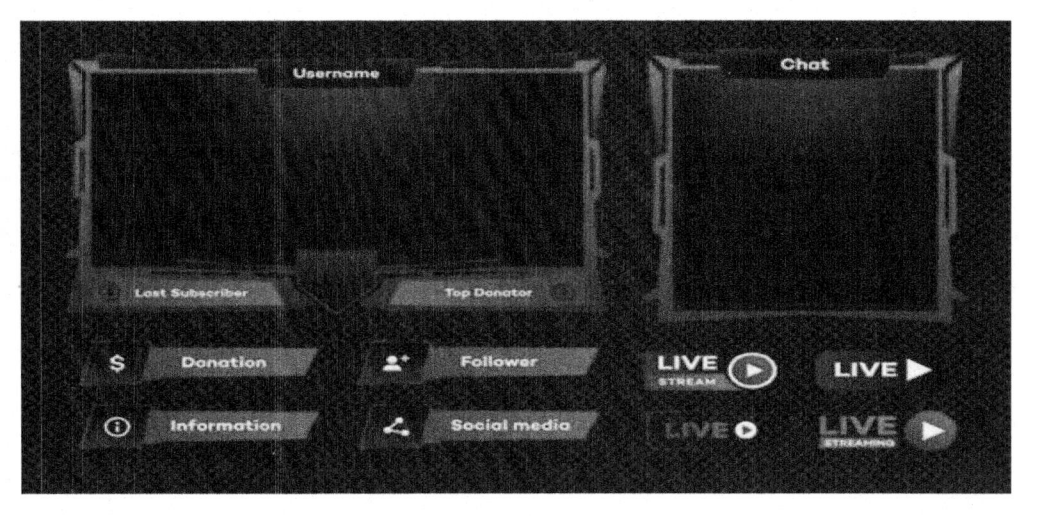

Starting in our Twitch channel means having to do certain things for your brand to remember your lighting in your room, a way of fully emphasizing your brand and who you are by having a great Twitch panel. Your panels are the first things that people will notice when they look at your channel. It's best to leave a great first impression. Therefore it would also be in your best interest to put information on what you and your channel are all about.

Simplifying what a panel is, it's basically where the general information regarding you and your streams is located. This organizes the information in your bio so that it's easier to read and browse through. Things like your contact information (your business email address), your steaming time, and your social media information should be in your panel. If you want to give your Twitch channel a more personal touch for your viewers, you could even add an about me panel that gives them a more in-depth feel of who you are and what you're about before even watching one of your streams.

Keep the information in your panels as straightforward as can be. You want to keep it short and sweet. For example, when you create your streaming schedule panel, just put the day and the time you intend on streaming. Keep in mind that it's best to adhere to the schedule that you set. The more consistent you are in streaming, the more likely you will gain followers and possibly gain sponsors!

Twitch Secrets: The Experts Guide To Become Twitch Partner

Circling back to panels, it's important to keep your designs similar to what you have going on with your branding. Keep the designs close to what you have on your overlays. The best way to achieve this is by keeping the color scheme and font style similar. But, if you're starting and want to have a hassle-free streaming experience, here's a list of where to get the best Twitch panel designs:

OWN3D.tv

Own3d has a collection full of Twitch panels that vary in designs so that you could pick and choose one that suits your style and branding. The best thing about them is that once you pick out your design, it can automatically be uploaded into OBS or SLOBS. But if you choose to edit and add some more details to the pre-existing design they offer, you could also download the files and edit them through Adobe Photoshop or any other editing softwares. They also offer free and animated Twitch panels that help bring your channel to life.

Here's a quick list of the pre-made panel categories that Own3d offers that could be downloaded as JPEG files:
- About
- Contact
- Discord
- Donate
- Facebook
- Giveaway
- Hardware
- Instagram
- Loots
- Rules
- Schedule
- Subscribe

Twitch Secrets: The Experts Guide To Become Twitch Partner

- Twitter
- YouTube.

Pro tip: Many of the panels offered are also included in packages designed and produced by Own3d. It would be more cohesive for your brand and easier for you for streaming if you choose to purchase packages. This way, you won't have to worry about the fluidity of your brand on your channel, and you know that you're showing professional-looking designs on your channel!

Nerd or Die

Like Own3d, Nerd or Die offers a wide variety of panel designs that also come in full packages. These are completely customizable, so you don't have to worry if you want something a little more personalized written on your panels.

If you fancy something more custom, Nerd or Die has a panel maker wherein you could create basic panel designs for free. You could customize the fonts, size, colors and add text to your panels. In this panel maker, you could even choose an icon for your designs! This is great for streamers who don't have editing softwares available on their setups and those who want something easily accessible. Not to mention this is a great choice for streamers who are just starting and want something that looks professionally made sans the costly price tag.

In addition to panels, Nerd or Die also offers stream alerts, Twitch overlays, sound effects, looping backgrounds, stream transitions, and stream deck key icons.

Placeit

Placeit is a database website where you could find some of the best editable graphics on the internet. There are about 13,000 mockups on the site, and around 50 of those are Twitch panels. You have the choice between purchasing the files one at a time or subscribing to Placeit with a monthly or yearly fee. With the subscription, you get to unlock great designs that you could use to build your brand on your Twitch channel. Through Placeit, you could edit the basic design concepts of panel categories you'll need, like its color, text, font and graphics.

Twitch Secrets: The Experts Guide To Become Twitch Partner

This is instantaneous, so you wouldn't have to wait for a designer to take note of what you want and wait a couple of hours to a few days to receive your design requests. Plus, this is great for new streamers who want to quickly set up their Twitch channels without compromising the quality of the designs of their panels.

Visuals by Impulse Twitch Panels

Visuals by Impulse offer a few free packs and some that are very reasonably priced. They offer 10 Twitch Panel designs that vary in styles and colors, and all of them are compatible with Twitch.

Their Twitch panel categories are as follows (not all are included in every package): about me, about us, apparel, contact us, Discord, donate, donations, F.A.Q, Facebook, PC-Specs, Instagram, playlist, rules, schedule, Snapchat, sponsors, stream graphics, subscribe, Twitter, and YouTube.

Aside from their ready-made designs, Visuals by Impulse offer custom graphics for very reasonable prices. These are professionally designed, and they work well with you to fully understand your concept designs to encapsulate your branding.

Small Streamers Free Twitch Panels

Support Small Streamers is a platform created to cater to small streamers to help them network and create a Twitch Team of a few people. The team doesn't accept many applications because they want to retain their high standards for those who want to network. Although, they do offer a selection of free resources that include free Twitch Panels.
They offer 31 sets of Twitch Panels in varying styles, albeit a lot of these are based on popular games. They don't offer the choice of editing the ready-made panels, but if all you need is a few categories from this list, they are readily available for download on their site. The categories are: about me, donate, rules, setup, Discord, gear, schedule, and subscribe. Some of the sets even offer more categories such as social media, FAQ, and rules.

Free Twitch Panels

Wdflat offers approximately 100 bundles of free Twitch panels on their site. A lot of these bundles include a video stipulating how the designs were created! Once you've chosen a design

Twitch Secrets: The Experts Guide To Become Twitch Partner

of your liking, all you have to do is to download the zip file and then upload the png files onto your Twitch channel. While there are multitudes of readily available designs on Wdflat, it is notable that these are not available for editing.

The categories included will vary from package to package. Still, it is safe to assume that the following can be found in the packages: about me, armoury, chat emotes, chat rules, Discord, donate, Facebook, FAQ, follow, G2A, goals, hall of fame, hardware, Instagram, loots, schedule, sponsors, Steam, stuff, subscribe, the top donator, Twitter, WDFLAT, website, and YouTube.

Remember that when you're looking for a Twitch panel design for your channel, there are several things that you have to consider. But, the one thing you have to be clear with is conveying the right understanding of your brand and your content, and the rest will follow.
To fully emphasize

Twitch Secrets: The Experts Guide To Become Twitch Partner

Dual PC Streaming Setup - Is It Worth It?

When streaming gameplay, a big factor you have to consider is whether or not your PC can handle the game you're playing and streaming simultaneously. Some games that are being produced nowadays push the limits of our PCs, and when we add streaming into the mix of things, things can go downhill really fast.

If your PC shows signs of struggling like lagging and freezing up while playing games and streaming, the best possible solution to your problem might just be upgrading to a dual-PC setup.

Although, if you're building his PC and purchasing part by part, it is best for you to just focus on building one PC that fits your needs instead of building two separate PCs. Having a dual-PC setup would require you to use other bits and pieces that could potentially alter the overall quality of your setup. In addition to this, screen tearing (shifting of an image on screen) could also be a problem because of the capture cards.

While it sounds like a great idea, let's discuss the necessity, the pros and cons of having a dual-PC setup, and how to set up a dual-PC setup with a capture card.

Do you need to have a dual-PC setup?

Twitch Secrets: The Experts Guide To Become Twitch Partner

Having a dual-PC setup is only truly needed when you play CPU-heavy games or operate CPU-heavy softwares. A lot of streamers don't need dual-PC setups. But If your PC struggles with performing when a game and a stream element are running, the lag can annoy you and your audience.

If that's the case, the thought of adding another PC to your setup could be tempting to relieve you and your primary PC of the stress of running heavy programs together. But, there are other options out there to consider before shelling out cash to buy another PC.

1. Before playing the game, you want to play and look up the specs it needs to play. There might just be some upgrades you can make to optimize the current setup to cater to its needs. Smaller upgrades mean less money spent.

2. Check out the game settings. Sometimes, games are automatically set to its highest setting, meaning it consumes more PC power than it needs. Adjusting the setting could spare you some PC power to allow you to stream without any hiccups. But, when you adjust this, you have to keep in mind what your viewers see when you're streaming as well. As much as possible, maintain the best quality you can push out for your viewers.

3. Sometimes, idle programs you forgot to close can take up a lot from your PC. It's best to ensure you've closed all programs that are not needed for your stream before you go live.

Twitch Secrets: The Experts Guide To Become Twitch Partner

4. Overclocking can help with increasing the speed of your PC. Although, tread lightly because this can cause damage to your hardware.

Pros of having a dual-PC setup:

1. Streaming wouldn't be an issue. You wouldn't have to worry about overheating your PC and whether or not you could stream longer. Your primary PC wouldn't beat up too much from using it for an extended period of time and running heavy softwares.

2. Better video quality for your streams is expected with this upgrade. You can now stream with a higher game setting, meaning you could stream with a 1080p resolution instead of 720p. You don't even have to worry about losing performance over this change. Although this is still dependent on your internet speed, it's best to have a good internet plan to stream at 1080p resolution.

3. More memory, more power, less lag!

4. Having two PCs makes it possible to have a multiple-camera source so that you could take shots at different angles. You could even have a pet cam for your fur baby's fans.

5. File management will be easier with two PCs because things will be more organized. Each PC would have its own file structure catered to your liking.

6. Two PCs mean more USB ports for your gaming and streaming equipment. You won't ever have to worry about not having enough ports for equipment.

7. There are days when the game just doesn't work the way it should, and you'd have to restart your PC. With a dual-PC setup, you wouldn't have to end your stream and restart it when you reboot your gaming PC. You wouldn't have to re-hype your stream.

Cons of having a dual-PC setup:

1. The noise. There would be two cooling fans running while you're streaming. With this, there is a high chance that there would be background noise while you're streaming. This is trivial, as you could just place it far enough from you and your microphone so that it wouldn't pick up the noise while streaming so as not to disrupt the audio quality.

Twitch Secrets: The Experts Guide To Become Twitch Partner

2. Setting this up would be such a hassle to do. To get it up and run, you'd have to put up cables to and from both PCs to make sure everything is integrated. On top of the hardware problems, you'd have to tinker around with other softwares to find out which applications to use to run on your primary and secondary PC.

3. It is expensive to run. Not only would you be worried about the cost of a second PC and capture card, but you'd have to worry about your electricity bill each month.

4. Screen tearing is a big possible issue. Screen tearing happens when the image on the screen seems to split. It happens randomly, regardless of whatever capture card is used. This could be minimized to some degree, but there have been cases wherein it wouldn't go away at all.

Now that we've talked about the pros and cons of having a dual-PC setup let's talk about how to set it up (should you decide to push through with having a dual-PC setup).

What do I need to set up a dual-PC setup?

In order to set up a dual-PC setup, at the very least, you would need 2 PCs, a capture card, and HDMI cables. In its simplest form, a dual setup requires you to route your primary gaming PC to your secondary streaming PC through your capture card. You'd have to connect each tower to its individual tower. It's best to have at least two monitor two for this set-up.

Capture cards can either be internal or external set-ups. Capture cards are best installed on the streaming PC. When installing your internal capture card, just follow the manufacturer's instructions and connect this to your gaming PC through an HDMI cable. Should you choose to get an external capture card, plug it into your streaming PC with the USB and then connect it to background and when the green screen is rolled inThe ensure that you have installed all the necessary drivers to make it function properly.

Once everything is properly set up, you could access the display settings on your gaming computer. Make sure that your capture card is working as a duplicate display.

After doing so, open your streaming software on your streaming computer and add the capture card as a video source in the program. Ensure that this is capturing the information from your gaming PC and that both the audio and visuals are coming through. You can do this by playing a video on your gaming PC and watching it on your streaming PC.

Twitch Secrets: The Experts Guide To Become Twitch Partner

Therefore, when the green screen is rolled in the room here are some few tips to remember when configuring your setup:

- The PC with a better GPU should be your gaming PC as it processes the main visual content of your stream.

- Your streaming PC must have a better CPU and a bigger RAM capacity

- Your microphone has to be plugged into your gaming computer

- The webcam has to be plugged into your streaming PC

- The capture card has to be run from the gaming PC to the streaming PC

Overall, having a dual-PC setup is only really feasible if you have a spare PC. It is more economically friendly for you to just invest in upgrading your PC's components to boost its capabilities instead of getting another one. But, if you are able and wouldn't mind setting up the other PC to your current rig, then, by all means, enjoy the high-quality gaming and have fun streaming!

Twitch Secrets: The Experts Guide To Become Twitch Partner

How to IRL Stream on Twitch?

When we think of Twitch, it's almost automatic that we associate it with gaming. But in reality, Twitch has so much more to offer than just gaming! There are several categories of content that content makers can dabble in and for viewers to consume. Some streams range from travelling to ASMR and simply sitting down and having a morning chat with a streamer. Twitch is a haven for anyone who wants to share a piece of their life with a community of like-minded people.

A huge niche of Twitch is *In Real Life* streamers, or better known as IRL Streamers. IRL streaming is a term coined for the act of broadcasting that doesn't involve video game content on streaming platforms like Twitch, YouTube Gaming, and Facebook Gaming. Typically, IRL streams cover activities such as travelling, arts and crafts, and just chatting.

How do I IRL Twitch Stream?

IRL Twitch streaming is fairly simple. Here are a few steps to follow for you to get started on your stream:

1. Before you start streaming, you have to create a plan on what activity you might want to do on stream. The best way to start your plan is to choose a category. It would be easier for you to be more natural if you choose a category that you're familiar with. It's more entertaining and pleasing to your audience if you're comfortable with what you're doing on stream!

Twitch Secrets: The Experts Guide To Become Twitch Partner

2. Once you've decided what you want to do, it's best to round up your equipment for the stream. Specific activities may need a multiple-camera set up to show your viewers a better angle of what you're trying to do. For example, if you're IRL streaming yourself cooking in the kitchen, it's best to have a secondary camera to highlight what you're doing with your hands, be it slicing or simply showing what you have cooking in the pot. If you plan to do something more outdoorsy, like a walk in the park or just around the block, it's best to ensure that you have the equipment that would beat the odds of nature. For example, having an external microphone with a windscreen to block the wind noise would be ideal if you're out on a windy day. On top of this, it's best to ensure you have excellent cell service to maintain the quality of your stream and avoid technical difficulties.

3. It's never a bad idea to practice! A practice run with your equipment is vital in making sure that everything is working seamlessly. In addition to this, when you do a test run, check the quality of the lighting in your venue of choice. It's not entertaining to see a silhouette talking.

4. Going back to a multiple-camera setup, it's best to look for good overlays for your stream. Adding an overlay to your stream is a bonus to your stream's entertainment value and overall branding. It's also best to check what other content creators use as an overlay for the IRL category you chose to see what works.

5. Apart from overlays, you should also set up your graphics and your Twitch alerts on the broadcasting software you have. Again, this is for added entertainment and branding value on your channel.

6. To make yourself more known to your viewers, fill in your Twitch about me section to discuss what your channel is about and what IRL categories you want to cover on your streams. Letting your viewers know what you want to do would entice viewers to subscribe to your channel to see your future content.

7. Now that you have covered the basics of your Twitch channel, it's time to go live!

Twitch Secrets: The Experts Guide To Become Twitch Partner

Do I need certain equipment?

The kind of equipment you'll need to IRL stream depends on the category of content you want to create. Know what you want to do first, and then plan how you're going to stream it. Breaking IRL streams down, they're all either streamed indoors or outdoors.

Here's a quick list of what you'll be needing for indoor streams:

- **A Camera** - as long as it can be connected to a broadcasting platform, you're good to go! You could use a webcam, a cell phone or a video camera.

- **Lights** - it's best to have good lighting while on stream. Cameras can only ever do so much for your appearance, but with good lighting, your video quality can be so much better.

- **Microphone** - investing in a high-quality microphone is ideal for your streams. It's more pleasing for the viewers to be watching a stream without much background noise.

- **Royalty-free Music** - the last thing you want to have is a copyright strike on your channel for playing copyrighted music during your downtime. The best place to find

Twitch Secrets: The Experts Guide To Become Twitch Partner

DMCA-free music is Epidemic Sound! Dodge the DMCA takedowns easily by playing copyright-free music.

- **Computer or Device** - when you start streaming, you need a computer or a laptop that would process your content to be sent to Twitch for your viewers to watch! It would be best if you have a high-performance computer to do so, as to avoid lag and other technical difficulties mid-stream.

Outdoor streams require more compact yet high-performing equipment. Here's a list of what you'll need:

- **Video Camera** - a lightweight camera that's not too fussy to carry around is ideal for streaming outdoors. It doesn't have to be super fancy. A lot of streamers just use their cellphones to stream!

- **Battery Packs** - there's no worse way to end a stream than a stream ending caused by a dead battery. Avoid this by keeping an extra battery pack or two handles when IRL streaming!

- **Computer or Device** - just like indoor streaming, you'll need a device that would process your content into Twitch to broadcast to your viewers! Just make sure that it's handy and not too heavy to be bringing along.

- **Cellular modems** - ensure you'll never have to face network issues by bringing cellular modems along for your streams. You won't be able to stream on Twitch if you have network issues!

- **Streaming Backpack** - having a backpack that's designated for streaming is ideal. It has to be big enough to carry all the things you need for your stream and compact enough for it not to be a bother to carry!

What are the Twitch IRL Categories?

IRL streaming used to be a category on its own. But as the number of IRL streamers rose, they got more creative with subcategories for IRL streaming, which became main categories for Twitch IRL. Here's a list of Twitch IRL's categories:

Twitch Secrets: The Experts Guide To Become Twitch Partner

- **Just Chatting** - this is the most general category in IRL streams. This covers almost anything unrelated to gaming and other specific topics. This is also one of the most popular categories on Twitch as a whole!

- **Music** - this is where musicians jam out and play covers and their original compositions to share with their viewers. Typically, the performers have a setlist, but they usually take in song requests from their viewers.

- **Special Events** - sometimes streamers throw or attend specific events that don't fall under a specific genre in IRL streaming categories. This is where they usually stream in those times.

- **Food and Drink** - foodies will revel in this category because this is where home cooks and the occasional professionals share their recipes and beverage mixes to their audience!

- **Talk Shows and Podcasts** - this is where people who have a knack for length conversations and TV Show ideas gather and share ideas!

- **Science and Technology** - some of the world's brightest minds talk about the ins and outs of scientific facts and technological advancements in the modern world.

- **ASMR** - otherwise known as *"Autonomous Sensory Meridian Response,"* takes you to creators who make content that would help you relax or fall asleep to whispers and soft sounds they make on their high-tech, ultra-sensitive microphones

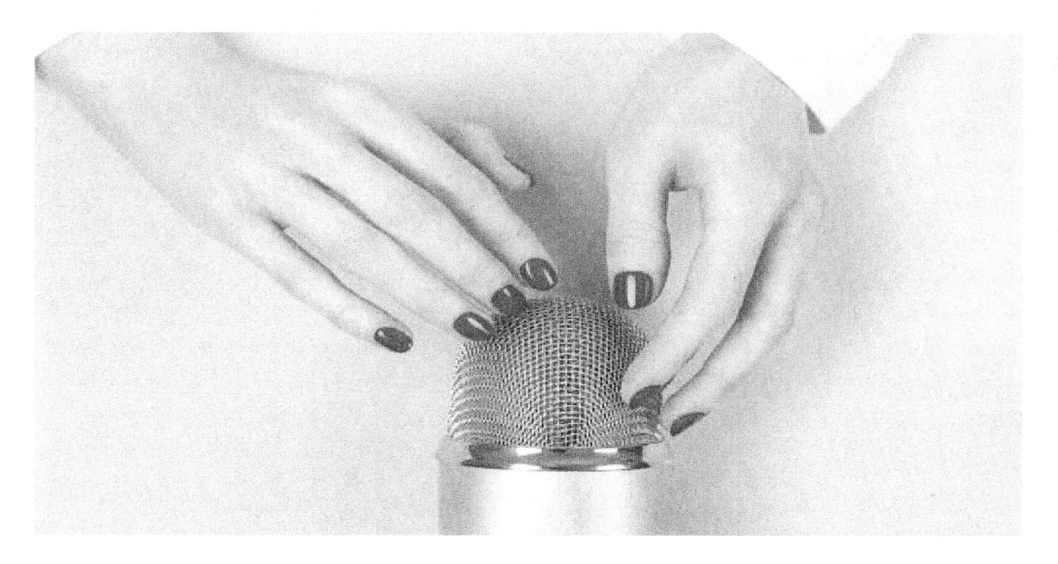

Twitch Secrets: The Experts Guide To Become Twitch Partner

- **Travel and Outdoors** - this is where people who love to explore and share their perspective of the world come to what they encounter while exploring to their viewers! This category lets you roam the world from the comfort of your own home.

- **Makers and Crafting** - the world's creative minds gather here to share their artistic points of view and their art while chatting to their viewers.

- **Sports** - this category covers explicitly anything related to sports (this category doesn't cover esports)

- **Fitness and Health** - here, you will find people who are passionate about health and fitness. You'll see streamers giving classes or exercising.

- **Politics** - if you're interested in a good debate or just trying to broaden your perspective on certain topics under politics, this category is for you.

- **Beauty and Body Art** - everything make-up, body art, and fashion are tackled in this category.

There are still uncategorized niches on Twitch. If what you want to do doesn't fit in with those listed here, don't feel pressured to feel like you have to conform to them. As long as you aren't breaking Twitch's ToS, you're free to create a community of your own!

Here are a few quick tips and reminders to have a successful IRL stream:

1. **Follow the regulations.** Remember to be respectful of the Twitch ToS and the local laws while you're streaming. Breaking the Twitch ToS can lead to you being banned from streaming on Twitch. Even worse, live broadcasting yourself breaking the law is Here self-incrimination.

2. **Cloudbots.** These are lifesavers for when you get FAQs about your stream. Set up your chatbot commands to allow the cloudbot to answer questions that might be repetitive. It's better to be focused on what you're doing (or trying to do) as opposed to answering the same question over and over again.

3. **High-quality graphics.** To maintain the overall quality of your stream, ensure that you have high-quality graphics to make your viewers feel like they're watching something professionally done. This would also help you with potentially getting sponsors in the future!

Twitch Secrets: The Experts Guide To Become Twitch Partner

4. **Find good moderators.** It's hard having to IRL stream and keep up with what's going on in your chat. Having good moderators to take care of your chat while doing what you're doing is such a big help in keeping things interesting for your viewers.

5. **Perfect the art of maneuvering your equipment.** You should be confident in how to use your equipment while live on-stream. This will give you the edge of looking and seeming incredibly calm and collected while troubleshooting technical difficulties you may have. Always remember to prioritize the quality of your stream and maintain that quality to build your brand!

Twitch Secrets: The Experts Guide To Become Twitch Partner

How to Simultaneously Stream on Twitch and YouTube

These days, streaming on multiple streaming platforms gives you an edge on how to broaden your horizon in terms of viewership. The thing is, some people prefer watching streams on one site as opposed to another. When you do the same content and stream it on two sites, you're killing two birds with one stone.

If you look at the trend of streamers nowadays, simultaneous streams are typically done by bigger streamers that are either partnered by certain brands or are freelance. But, we have to change the notion that only big streamers can do that. As a small streamer, you have to think outside the box to attract a bigger audience to your streams, and this might be the answer to a better, more viewed stream.

When streaming, it can feel like you're failing when your viewer count is low. That shouldn't bother you, because we have to start somewhere, right?

Streaming on multiple platforms ensures you pull from different pools of audiences every time you stream. This means you can urge and push different people to follow you on your social media accounts and your channel itself!

Twitch Secrets: The Experts Guide To Become Twitch Partner

Multistreaming also ensures you that your growth is tied down to one channel only. This means that when the time comes that one platform is down, the other channels you have won't be taking the same dip. For example, there are times that YouTube's streaming services are down. If you only had YouTube Gaming for streaming, you wouldn't be able to stream for that day, or however long it takes to get the servers up and going again. If you streamed on multiple platforms, you wouldn't lose the platform's downtime to grow your channel.

With continuous streaming, your channel's growth would shoot up. The more views you have, the more chances for you to get sponsors for your channel. This could either be a sponsorship or affiliate program. If the odds are in your favor, gaming sponsors are more likely to follow your work and eventually work with you.

Now that we've discussed the pros of simultaneously streaming on multiple platforms, let's focus on the technicalities.

Is multistreaming allowed on Twitch?

Twitch is quite strict with multistreaming. Twitch doesn't appreciate it when their content creators stream to multiple platforms at the same time. If you try to do so, you might have to kiss being an affiliate or partner goodbye. A loophole to this is streaming on different platforms at different times. Another way is to upload content like clips and the like on YouTube 24 hours after the steam ended.

Things get trickier once you are a monetized streaming account because they are legally bound to not stream on other platforms. Although, if you wanted to, you could stream on embedded sites or platforms that weren't built for streaming. You must read and understand what is written on your platform's rules to know what is and isn't allowed. A lot of streamers got permission to stream on other platforms by looking for the loopholes in their agreements.

Should I Multi-stream to Facebook?

Facebook Gaming is on the rise due to the downfall of *Mixer,* a streaming platform. With *Mixer*'s downfall came the rise of Facebook Gaming due to former streamers on *Mixer* moving on to greener pastures with Facebook Gaming. Despite this, it is still fairly easy to grow a community with Facebook Gaming because many people are looking for new people to watch streams.

Twitch Secrets: The Experts Guide To Become Twitch Partner

Should I Multi-Stream on YouTube?

YouTube offers a broad reach when it comes to searches and finding audiences. It is the second-largest search engine in the world. The game streaming side of YouTube is still quite young as compared to other streaming platforms. But, the success rates of those who made it on YouTube gaming have been high (i.e.: Vikkstar123, Pewdiepie, Lachlan). Not to mention that the community is growing year in and out.

Are There Cons to Multistreaming?

Technically, it is against the Terms of Service of the platform if this monetizes you. What does this mean? If you're earning money from the stream you're doing, be it a sponsored item you're using or anything that you benefit from on-stream, it isn't allowed to multi-stream and is grounds for suspension. A great example of this is how Twitch Affiliates cannot show content streamed through Twitch on other platforms within 24 hours of ending the stream.

As mentioned earlier, if you choose to maximize all platforms, it's best to manage your time wisely to allow yourself to learn about other platforms and stream on other platforms. In addition to this, you'd have to plan on the logistics of how you will promote yourself on that platform because what works for platform A won't necessarily work for platform B. Small variances have a big impact on your overall quality of work.

With this, you might have a hard time creating a community. For example, you're streaming on Twitch and YouTube Gaming. The Twitch community might be saying something entirely different for the YouTube community. If that's the case, it will create a big disconnect between the two, wherein you're trying to make just one general community.

And, let's not forget the technical aspect of it. Things might be going smoothly for one platform, but things could be completely different for another. Small things like disconnection, audio lag, drop frames, and the like are bound to happen.

But, if you don't mind having to deal with minor cons like this, here is how to stream to both YouTube and Twitch for free.

How to Multi-stream for Free!

Twitch Secrets: The Experts Guide To Become Twitch Partner

Streaming on multiple platforms is made easier with Restream. Although, using the free version of Restream means having to use their watermark. Here is the step by step guide on using Restream to multi-stream:

1. Create a Restream account. You will need a unique username, password and a valid e-mail address.

2. Choose which platforms you want to stream on. Restream supports various platforms like Twitch, Facebook, YouTube, Twitter, Linkedin and 30+ more.

3. Select which plan offered suits your needs better. Restream is free, but you wouldn't be able to record or store streams and show the Restream branding. If you would rather have the watermark removed, you could upgrade to a professional subscription. But, if you're only starting, it's best for you to just stick with the free version first.

4. Once you've chosen your plan, connect your channels. Click on the platform icon and connect your social media accounts with Restream.

5. With the minor details done, you can not set up your broadcasting preferences and streaming software. You could choose to stream directly from your browser, have multiple participants in different locations, from a phone or GoPro, or you could even choose to stream directly into your website.

Aside from Restream, you could also multi-stream with Streamlabs Prime. This is the premium addition to Streamlabs that gives you access to 40 different apps that improve your streaming quality and could earn you more money through merch sales. With Streamlabs Prime, you could use multi stream from SLOBS. It's one of the best streaming softwares on the market.

Another option is MelonApp, a browser streaming software that Streamlabs made to cater to professionals who need to start streaming as part of their career. It was made during the 2020 pandemic when office work started to shift to working from home. This is easy to set up and gives you many simple options to create a seamless stream straight from your browser. The premium version of this lets you stream on many other platforms with just a single click.

Twitch Secrets: The Experts Guide To Become Twitch Partner

Starting your streaming career by multi-streaming is tedious work, but it will be worth it in the end. That is if you don't mind the added work it entails. It's best to stream on the big streaming platforms (Twitch, Facebook Gaming and YouTube Gaming) if you're looking to grow your audience.

If you choose to stream on multiple platforms simultaneously, let your viewers know that you're streaming on more than one site to avoid confusion. Communication is important when trying to entertain more than one group of people at the same time. If you find yourself liking and leaning towards one streaming platform as opposed to the others, tell your viewers this information so that those who are interested in watching more of your content could follow you to that channel.

The best thing for you to do is to wait till you've reached a pretty decent-sized community before signing on as a Twitch Affiliate or any other partnership. Remember that you would be signing on to cutting back from streaming on other streaming platforms by doing so. If you have already signed on but still want to stream on other platforms, remember to stream on different days to respect the agreement you made.

Multistreaming is not something for the faint of heart. But remember that consistency is key when streaming. Whether or not you decide to multistream, remaining consistent on the quality of the streams you make is important in keeping your viewers interested and satisfied.

Twitch Secrets: The Experts Guide To Become Twitch Partner

How to Stream on Facebook Gaming

Various social media sites have now adapted to the new in-trend of streaming: Gaming. Gameplay streams have been very popular with the rise of gaming clans such as FaZe and Optic in the *Call of Duty* and *Counter-Strike* era and the individual streamers such as Ninja and Pewdiepie.

Traditionally, gameplay streams were broadcasted on sites such as YouTube and Twitch, but recently. Still, recently eased their gameplay streaming service when they caught on to the number of streamers and content Twitch was producing. A lot of streamers struck luck with Facebook Gaming, such as AverageDad and ZLaner.

Getting started with Facebook Gaming is quick and easy.

Set up your Facebook Gaming Creator Page

Before anything else, you have to set up your Facebook Gaming Creator Page to create the actual page where you stream. To create the page, you must first log on to the gaming page creator section on Facebook and create a page.

Twitch Secrets: The Experts Guide To Become Twitch Partner

The next thing you have to do is to upload a profile picture. It would be best to have your logo at this point, so you could establish your brand instantly to the people who will be watching your Streams. For added personalization to your page, don't forget to add a description. Information such as a business email, your manager's or your management team's information (if you are under a management team) should be stipulated there to contact you for future collaborations and the like easier for the future when PR teams want to reach you.

Once you have your page set up and are happy with its overall look, you can share your page and invite your friends to like and join your page.

Now that the easy part of the job is done let's tackle the more technical parts of streaming.

Third-party streaming softwares for better streams

Nowadays, when you check tig streamers' content, we see that their video feed is very customized. We could see the presence of chatbots, stream alerts and their branding while playing games. This is all customizable through streaming softwares.

OBS, SLOBS and XSplit are compatible third-party streaming softwares that are common in today's streaming styles. They offer a levelled-up streaming experience for both you and your audience because of the easy customization they offer.

Twitch Secrets: The Experts Guide To Become Twitch Partner

Streamlabs OBS

The beginner-friendly third-party streaming software is Streamlabs OBS (also known as SLOBS). This has been dubbed as the best streaming software by many loyal streamers. Streamlabs OBS was made to be easy to use and even easier to navigate than its competitors. It has also been highly commended due to its versatility. They even offer an "all-star program" wherein you could unlock exclusive rewards as your channel grows.

Installing Streamlabs OBS is very simple. All you have to do is visit the Streamlabs website and download the free software. Once the software has been installed into your computer, you could sync the program with your Facebook account.

An easy way to sync your Facebook account to Streamlabs is simply signing in to Facebook on Streamlabs itself. It should automatically sync your accounts so that you will be able to stream automatically without any problems. But, if for some reason you're having a hard time linking your Facebook account to Streamlabs, you might have to input your stream key into Streamlabs manually.

Why Streamlabs OS?

Streamlabs OS has built its reputation as the easiest to use and set up streaming software. Aside from SLOBS being incredibly beginner friendly, it is also equally as versatile.

Twitch Secrets: The Experts Guide To Become Twitch Partner

As beginner streamers, you would want every stream to go as seamlessly as possible, and with SLOBS' features, this is achievable with just a few clicks. Features like the cloudbot, widgets, support and updates are readily available to make setting up your streams and streaming itself easier for you and your audience.

Finding Your Facebook Stream Key

As mentioned before, finding your Facebook stream key if you're having a hard time syncing your accounts. Find your Facebook stream key, log onto your Facebook Live page and clock the *"Create Live Stream"* button. On the right-hand, click on *"Share on a Page You Manage"* on the drop-down menu from the *"Choose Where to Post Your Broadcast"* box.

After that, choose your Facebook Gaming page. Then, input the game category and create a stream title. You could then copy the stream key from the page. Once you have the stream key, you can then open your streaming software and paste the stream key in the appropriate settings. If you did all the steps properly, you could now go live on Facebook through your streaming software.

Stream Screens Set Up

Screens are the banners you have for the general theme of what you're doing at the moment. It isn't all the time that you will be streaming a game. There is the build-up, build-up where you start your stream and allow a certain amount of time for your audience to trickle in, the *"Just Chatting"* screen, where you just talk to your chat, and it will be highlighted on your screen. These usually go hand-in-hand with your brand, typically with the design and the color scheme style.

But, if you want to take things easy and have something premade and readily available to use, there are several places you can look at to find the Facebook Gaming scenes you want to use.

- OWN3D has several packs (both discounted and premium) available. The graphics in the packs offered have all things you need to quickly set up for your channel so that you could achieve the style and interface you want.

Twitch Secrets: The Experts Guide To Become Twitch Partner

- Placeit offers professionally animated scenes that would match your chosen color scheme. The great thing about Placeit is how you can opt to edit in certain information that would better suit your brand.

- Streamlabs Prime offers great scene templates, and you can edit them to make them go with the overall brand you have.

Editing your SLOBS scenes is fairly easy. You would just have to select each source in the source boxes and edit them individually. In addition to this, you could even upload more sources to give the scenes a more personalized look.

The most basic scene is the *"Just Chatting"* scene, which is used at the beginning and end of streams to greet and chat a bit with your viewers. The *"Content"* scene typically shows your content with a webcam box in a corner, and usually, this is where widgets detailing the most recent followers and subscribers are located. The most under-appreciated scene - the *"BRB"* scene - is the one you use when you need a quick break mid-stream. It tells your viewers that you're AFK and will be back in a bit.

Transitions between scenes will add a more professional touch to your entire stream production. Streamlabs can do this, but if you choose to stream more consistently or maybe even professionally, investing in the Elgato Stream Deck would help you streamline, making faster transitions between scenes with just a push of a button.

Facebook Gaming has been slowly but surely establishing itself as a big competitor towards Twitch, YouTube Gaming and the like. Now is a great time to start building your platform with Facebook Gaming because they are still on the rise, and it's great to establish yourself as one Of the first streamers to make their mark on the platform. Here are a few additional little tips to help boost your streaming page:

Add Overlays and Graphics

By doing so, you're fully cementing your branding across your stream, making the mental recall of your audience easier. It makes your content feel more thought-of, and potential sponsors would take you more seriously if your present screams professionalism.

Twitch Secrets: The Experts Guide To Become Twitch Partner

Be articular with your mic and audio for streaming.

Always aim for the best production you can have for every stream. This means having the best microphone to produce the best audio for the stream. Choose a microphone that blocks background noise but is crisp when intaking audio. Think of it this way. You wouldn't want to watch someone streaming with bad audio, so why would you incorporate that into your brand, right?

The same rules apply to your webcam, greenscreen and lighting.

Again, you have to aim for the best. In streaming, your visuals and audio are the main things you have to look out for. We already talked about audio, but it doesn't stop with the quality you stream with for visuals. You have to consider that you're going to be steaming with your camera on at some point. A lot of viewers love it when they can see the reaction of the streamers as they play a game or a video, therefore having a pristine quality webcam, lighting and greenscreen is the best thing to have. This doesn't necessarily mean breaking the bank for the best gear, as there are many cheap but quality equipment options in the market (which will be discussing many chapters).

Build your Facebook Gaming Community

Your first few streams are you dipping your toe in the water. You have to get a feel of what it's like before you plunge in headfirst. Be in tune with what your viewers say and take the feedback as constructive criticism. Improve as you go. There's no other way to grow.

The only way to truly grow your community is to be consistent with your streams. Set a schedule, whatever is comfortable with you and just let things flow. Hear out your audience, what do they want to see? What do they want to try out with you? What games are trending at the moment? Start from there, and the rest will eventually follow.

Always be kind

You have a platform and are responsible for teaching and inspiring people to become better people for society. Don't forget to thank your viewers for spending their time with you while you stream.

Make sure everything is switched off after streaming

This goes without saying, but there have been way too many instances of people forgetting to turn off their cameras or their microphones and have gotten banned for accidentally displaying certain acts/content against streaming rules.

Twitch Secrets: The Experts Guide To Become Twitch Partner

How to Subscribe on Twitch?

The most common way that Twitch Affiliates and Partners gain revenue from streaming is by gaining Twitch subscriptions from their viewers. Viewers across Twitch's platform are able to subscribe to any and all channels that they choose in exchange for that channel's emotes and other things that the streamers set up for them.

What is a Twitch Sub, and How Much Does it Cost?

A Twitch sub is the act of paying for a subscription from your channel of choice. On Twitch, subscriptions come in three different tiers at three different price points introduced in 2017. Tier one costs $4.99, tier two at $9.99 and tier three is priced at $24.99. Most built-in features are available to all tiers, but having a tier two subscription offers you one extra remote, while tier three adds a bonus of two emotes to your collection.

Although, it still depends on the person you are subscribed to on what they offer on their channels. A lot of streamers put down these additional features on their "About Me."

Subscriptions can be charged monthly, quarterly (every three months), or bi-annually (every six months). All of which is renewed on the same date each month. For example, if you chose to subscribe to someone's channel on the 22nd of December and chose to pay quarterly, you will get billed on the 22nd of March, exactly three months after subscribing from that channel.

Twitch Secrets: The Experts Guide To Become Twitch Partner

Can I get a Twitch Subscription for Free?

If you have an Amazon Prime subscription, the good news for you is you can subscribe to Twitch channels with Prime Gaming! By simply connecting the two accounts, you get a free Twitch sub! Your Prime Gaming account is automatically counted as a $4.99 or a tier-one subscription. You must actively renew this every month, though.

How can I subscribe to a Twitch Channel from my desktop computer?

There are three very simple steps in order to subscribe to a Twitch Channel from a desktop computer. Here they are:

1. Simply go ahead and click on the Affiliated or Partnered channel of your liking. Next, click on the *subscribe* button located at the top right of the video player.

2. Next, a pop-up box should appear to show you and let you know the benefits of tier one, two, and three subscriptions. Simply click subscribe on the appropriate type of subscription you want to be a part of, and then click continue.

3. You will then be redirected to a page where you can pay with either PayPal or Credit Card. Click on *More Methods* and look for additional payment types or select a longer subscription time (assuming you chose tier one or two). Your subscription will begin as soon as the transaction has been processed. Most streamers who gain subscribers send a little thank you for their support.

Twitch Secrets: The Experts Guide To Become Twitch Partner

Is it possible to change a Twitch Sub to a different tier?

The type of Twitch Subscription you choose can be changed at any given time, should you choose to change it. But, it is noteworthy that if you choose to change your subscription type, the change happens automatically. It's best to change the type of subscription you have towards the end of the current one you have to avoid unnecessary spending and also, in order to get your money's worth from the first subscription type you chose.

Then change the subscription amount, go back to the channel of your choice and then hit the subscribe button once more. Another pop-up box will appear. It will likely give you the option of gifting subscriptions or looking at *All Paid Tiers*. Click on the latter option and then select the tier of your choice.

You're allowed to switch tiers even if you used Prime Gaming to subscribe to the channel originally. although, the new subscription will likely cost you money. Your subscription period will not start over.

Am I allowed to cancel my Twitch Subscription?

Let's be real, there will come a time that you might want to cancel on your subscription. When this time comes, it's just as easy to unsub as it was to sub to the channel. Simply click the avatar on the top-right of the screen from your Twitch account. Click on "subscriptions," from the

Twitch Secrets: The Experts Guide To Become Twitch Partner

Dropdown menu. A list of all your subscriptions should appear on that page. Simply select the subscription you want to cancel and then select the "don't renew" option.

What is there to gain from getting a Twitch Subscription?

The most significant gain in subscribing is giving and showing support to that specific streamer you subscribed to. Although, aside from the moral act of support, you get exclusive perks for gifting your favorite streamers a small monthly fee.

- **Ad-free Viewing.** With subscribing to your favorite streamer, you automatically get rid of the pesky ads you see during the broadcast. Although there are a certain few exceptions that Twitch has enforced on its platform, subscribing to a channel visually decreases the number of ads you see.

- **Sub-Badges.** The streamer fully customized these badges, and these change periodically. Those changes are dependent on your subscriptions streak. You get a 1-month badge, then 3, then 6, then nine and then one year!

- **Emotes.** Otherwise known as emoticons or emojis, Twitch Streamers can set up special emotes for their channel. The number of emotes they have is directly proportional to the number of subscribers that the streamers have amassed. The best thing is, you're not only limited to using those emotes on the streamer's channel, but you could also use it across Twitch! On top of that awesome fact, if the channel has a Discord server linked to it, you could also use the emotes on Discord as well!

- **Sub-only Chats/Streams.** Occasionally, Twitch Streamers would broadcast streams that are only allowed to be seen by their subscribers. Not only that, but the streamer also has the choice of setting their chat to "subscribers only." This is a great way for streamers to keep trolls at bay because the only people who can chat and participate in their stream chat are their subscribers.

- **Exclusive Chat Room on Discord.** This is just a bonus that some streamers offer to their subscribers. Many streamers offer this but not all of them. This varies from channel to channel.

- **Special Play Days.** Some streamers would set special days aside wherein they play games with their subscribers! If your ultimate goal is spending a day streaming with your favorite streamer, then subscribing to their channel is the best way to go about this goal. This would also be a great debut for you to showcase your talent and skills at gaming and potentially boost your channel.

Twitch Secrets: The Experts Guide To Become Twitch Partner

- **Competitions/Giveaways.** There will be times that streamers will conduct giveaways for their subscribers. This typically occurs around holidays or their birthdays as a form of them giving back to their fans.

- **Stream Alerts.** All streamers are extremely thankful for your support of their channel most of the time. They showcase those who have subscribed to them on stream through pop-up stream alerts. With this, you'll have your name displayed on Your favorite streamer's broadcast for a couple of seconds as a thank you for your support.

Overall, subscriptions are just an extra way to show your support to your favorite streamer. It isn't something that you are required to do just to show that you care for that particular streamer!

Streamers, in general, put a lot of work, time, and money to produce the streams that they have on their channels. Subscriptions are merely a way for viewers and real fans to encourage streamers, especially the new ones, to continually show their appreciation and offer a little financial support to allow the streamer to make and produce better content.

Twitch Secrets: The Experts Guide To Become Twitch Partner

Royalty-Free Music for Twitch

A huge rookie mistake for new streamers nowadays is not being as well-versed at the music-playing rules of Twitch. The thing is, Twitch has a strict set of guidelines with regards to the songs one is allowed to play on-stream. Negligence to the said guidelines can lead to your content being taken down from the site or worse, the permanent banning of your account from ever streaming on the platform.

Twitch isn't the only platform on the internet that has strict rules with the music policy. For example, YouTube is very particular with their music policy and non-compliance with their community guidelines could earn you a strike on your account.

DMCA takedowns happen all the time. This is because of AI programs that scan content being uploaded onto the internet for copyright music. Even a couple of seconds from a copyright-protected song could cause you so much trouble if you upload it on the internet.

With streaming, it's just not the same without music, especially when you're just chatting and hanging around with your subscribers on chat. Here's a good list of DMCA free music sources where you can play copyright-free music while on-stream.

Twitch Secrets: The Experts Guide To Become Twitch Partner

Epidemic Sound

Many streamers swear by Epidemic Sound to help boost the mood of their streams without the copyright strike. Epidemic Sound offers over 30,000 tracks of royalty-free music across several different genres and is compatible with Spotify.

They even make your life easier for uploading content onto YouTube because, through their program, you could simply select and download a part of a track to lay it on top of your video content while editing. Also, you could create your playlist and Twitch sound alerts with the audio clips you collect.

They offer a very affordable plan that covers music for YouTube, Facebook, Instagram and Twitch. They even throw in a free 30-day trial that allows you to explore and feel around the application before fully committing to its services.

Epidemic Sounds have the right to all of the music on their platform. And, you wouldn't have to worry about the songs being redundant because they add new tracks every week.

With a subscription with Epidemic Sounds, you wouldn't have to worry about DMCA takedowns. They work closely with the artists and producers of the music uploaded to their platform, and (legally speaking), Epidemic Sounds own all the music on their site. The only way you could ever get a copyright strike from them is if you used music from their site without having a subscription. To avoid this, simply link your channel to Epidemic Sounds to avoid the hassle of proving your subscription to Epidemic Sounds.

Twitch Secrets: The Experts Guide To Become Twitch Partner

OWN3D Music

Aside from all the high-quality graphics that Own3d offers, they also offer a music program specifically for streamers. Own3d has created over 200 LoFi and Synthwave sounds to cater to streamers who need copyright-free music for their streams.

Songs coming from the eight albums that Own3d has released are completely copyright-free, with no strings attached when using them. They're also working on adding more to their collection of music periodically, so their collection will only ever grow as time progresses, so you wouldn't have to worry about getting tired of the same old songs that go over and over again on your streams.

Envato Elements

Envato Elements has truly outdone itself by being the ultimate one-stop shop for many of our branding needs. With over 72,000 royalty-free songs, you're bound to get lost in a (copyright-free) musical trance while streaming. On top of this, they also offer over half a million royalty-free sound effects!

Once you find the music that you like, you could download the files or add it to a collection so you could go back to it later. You can also add and delete several collections if you want to keep things more organized.

Twitch Secrets: The Experts Guide To Become Twitch Partner

New streamers will appreciate Envato Elements' membership not only because of how easy it is for you to find royalty-free music. Also, because of their wide assortment of stock videos, video templates, graphic/social media templates, and so much more! These are some of the basic tools to help you build your brand while maintaining a clean and professional overall look.

Comma Music - Award-Winning Music

Comma Music grants you access to multitudes of tracks and sorts them by genre and style. The best part about this is how they are the only royalty-free music library that offers a student plan for their subscription price. You can easily create playlists for your Twitch streams and other traditional content creation purposes.

You won't have to worry about using their music for monetized content, as they have been cleared for it. They work with top composers and producers to create the best royalty-free music for many types of content. Many well-known brands have used their services to create advertisements or event music featuring their very own music.

They are very flexible with their subscription plans, as they offer many types of plans depending on your goals for the music and where you are in life. Occasionally, they offer discounts if you agree to subscribe to their services for a year or more. Just like a wholesale bargain!

Artlist

Being an Artlist member, you are ensured that you can download unlimited music for your streams. Multiple different major companies trust them. You can use their music on several different platforms, like Twitch and other social media sites, to build a cohesive brand for yourself.

Twitch Secrets: The Experts Guide To Become Twitch Partner

Artlist offers three possible plans for when you choose to become a member of their unlimited music subscription. Artlist is not known to copyright claim videos or any form of content you make with their music as long as you subscribe to their Music and SFX plan on their platform. They also upload new music on a daily basis, which allows you to always have something new to listen to on-stream.

Regarding Jingle Punks Music on Streamlabs Prime

With a premium plan on Streamlabs Prime, you can have access to Jingle Punks Music and their collection of over 100,000 songs in over a hundred categories. The music is professionally produced and audibly mimics the genre of your choosing. With this, you have the choice between a pre-made playlist, or you could create your very own playlists for your streams.

This app was made to truly cater to streamers, as you can customize your notifications for your stream when the song changes in the app itself. There's also the option of setting up the music to be played for the audience while you hear nothing at all. This is great for times where you're gaming, and you want to focus on what you're doing, like if you're looking out for in-game sounds or having a conversation over Discord.

There are a lot of avenues for you to find royalty-free music for your streams. There are even YouTube channels that cater to that specifically. Comfi Beats on YouTube uploads music that streamers can use for their streams. All Lili Pichu, the creator of Comfi Beats, asks is to give her credit for the music.

Twitch Secrets: The Experts Guide To Become Twitch Partner

Always remember to be careful with the music you play while on-stream. And as much as possible, double-check if it is royalty-free to avoid copyright strikes.

Twitch Secrets: The Experts Guide To Become Twitch Partner

The Best Streaming Software for Twitch

There are a lot of technical things that go on behind a stream. As much as possible, you would want to provide your audience the best quality content that you can push out. Picking a streaming software for your streams is totally vital to the overall quality of your streams. It is through streaming softwares that you are able to put on effects, transitions, and overlays.

Picking a streaming software for Twitch is completely reliant on what you need. You would want to find something that is relatively easy for you to use, would keep up with you, and one that you could keep up with during streaming.

Nowadays, tons of options out there can be a little overwhelming to a newbie streamer. When getting a streaming software, you have to look out for its ability to pull from several feeds that would give you a high-quality, professional-looking broadcast. Aside from this, a capture card-friendly software that offers great video quality and user support is a huge plus side.

Here, we will discuss some of the most highly recommended streaming softwares for Twitch that streamers rave about and highly recommend.

Streamlabs OBS

Twitch Secrets: The Experts Guide To Become Twitch Partner

Streamlabs OBS, better known as SLOBS, was heavily inspired by OBS. SLOBS was created in order to have software with a more accessible UI that could seamlessly integrate with other Streamlabs widgets and bots. Streamers using SLOBS speak highly of their easy-to-install plug-ins, such as their event queue, their collection of overlays, audio filters, and video editor.

Streamlabs OBS is customizable and is similar enough to OBS that if one chooses to switch over from SLOBS to OBS as their streaming software, they wouldn't have too rough of a time with getting to know the software a little bit more.

A notable thing about SLOBS is how some streamers believe that this software takes up more CPU and memory than other broadcasting softwares out there. While this may be true, they also state that it is, in fact, always improving. With this, it's also great to point out that Streamlabs OBS has impeccable customer service, who could aid you in understanding the settings, video and sound output and input, and other studio settings you should need.

Streamlabs OBS is free streaming software, but it also offers a Prime membership wherein you can gain access to so many features that would help you improve your channel. Things like 40+ premium apps, a merch store, a selection of overlays and such, and the choice to create a personalized website for your channel through their store are just a few of the many things you could get when you get a Prime membership with Streamlabs OBS.

OBS Studio

OBS - also known as Open Broadcaster Software - is quite literally the parent of Streamlabs OBS. It's also known to be the standard streaming software for regular Twitch streamers. OBS Studio is free and customizable, and it is open-source, which makes custom plug-ins easier to install onto your computer. It's best to tinker around with this to perfect your transitions and truly achieve that professional quality stream you want to achieve.

OBS comes with a select few inbuilt transitions to get you started. You can add to this. There's also the option of adding hotkeys to your setup to ensure every function has a key you could press, and it would work out as smooth as butter.

OBS doesn't have a centralized customer help center since this was a community project. But, since it was built by a community of amazing people, you won't have a hard time asking anyone for help. You can easily get an answer by just asking someone who's been using OBS for a long time. Everyone is happy to help!

Twitch Secrets: The Experts Guide To Become Twitch Partner

This has been tried and tested by streamers. They rarely run into any problems with this software. It's fully customizable, has many widgets and add ons, and is free. Albeit, it isn't the easiest software for beginner streamers, a lot of streamers have chosen to grow with it and have not looked at other streaming softwares after feeling the satisfaction of using OBS.

XSplit

Xsplit is best for all the beginner and growing channels on Twitch. This is the baby's first step into professional production quality streams! One thing that separates XSplit from Streamlabs OBS and OBS is how different the UI is from them. Thus users having to make adjustments with having to learn the software and such.

Just like SLOBS and OBS, this is completely customizable and comes complete with everything you'd need for your streams to get going. As mentioned earlier, there is a learning curve before fully getting things up and going with XSplit, but on the bright side, they have such a lovely customer support system that you wouldn't mind asking all the questions you need to ask and getting them all answered as you work.

There's a limited version of XSplit, which is free but has its watermark on display when you stream. But they offer a premium version of the software, which enables you to have full access to all of their bits and bobs.

Twitch Secrets: The Experts Guide To Become Twitch Partner

Gamecaster

Another beginner streamer-friendly software. This was formerly an extension of XSplit, but Gamecaster has broken out of its shell since stepping out of its beta phase. For beginners looking for a program that simply allows you to go on and get going, this one's for you.

This was created for new streamers by those who have more experience. They used all the knowledge they've gained from streaming to produce something that gives you everything you need to get started with streaming. The UI enables you to have a great interface that allows you to create scenes that let you stream content that your audience would highly appreciate. Gamecaster allows you to import multiple sources to give you a just-right look for your genre.

One setback to this amazing software is its inability for users to upload their branding. This is free software that gives you everything you need, from overlays to graphics to alerts and scene options. But, unfortunately, it does not allow you to upload your branding. The only way you can customize your setup is by using the things they have provided.

There are so many things you have to consider when getting streaming software for Twitch. Every streamer's needs are unique. A great example is how many streamers don't want or need 4K capabilities and would rather have a more affordable setup and less memory and CPU consumption. You have to hit many learning curves to find what's right for you, but you have to keep persevering and keep an eye peeled for something that suits you. In no time, you'll have a setup that allows you to create your smooth transitions of choice and effects that will hopefully put you up there with the unique and familiar names of great Twitch streamers.

Twitch Secrets: The Experts Guide To Become Twitch Partner

Twitch Secrets: The Experts Guide To Become Twitch Partner

Twitch Secrets: The Experts Guide To Become Twitch Partner

What Are Your Goals?

Realistic goals for 3 to 5 months from now:

Realistic goals for 12 months from now:

If it was easy, everybody would be there already...
What do you have to do to have the dream you want?

Twitch Secrets: The Experts Guide To Become Twitch Partner

NOTES:

Twitch Secrets: The Experts Guide To Become Twitch Partner

Thank You For Reading

I truly hope you enjoyed this guide and that it helps you achieve your set goal for your gaming career.

Sometimes the road we as Gamers travel on is a lonely road with people who don't believe in you, believe your wasting your time and those who hate on everything you do <u>no matter what you do!</u>

Always believe in yourself and use negativity as the fuel to keep you on the straight line to success. **Making Money Playing Video Games Is Possible!**

<u>There are 3 kinds of people:</u>

People who want things to happen…
People who make things happen…
People who just stand there, like.. "what the hell just happened?"

What kind of person are you?

Follow Me

Twitch: *swiissjokr*
Twitter: *swiissjoker*
Discord: *swiissjoker*
YouTube: *swiissjoker*

Printed in Great Britain
by Amazon